はしがき

　本書は第一学習社発行の英語教科書「CREATIVE English Communication I」に完全準拠したノートです。各パート見開き 2 ページで，主に教科書本文の予習や授業傍用での使用に役立つよう工夫しました。

CONTENTS

本書の構成と利用法

　本書は教科書本文を完全に理解するための学習の導きをしています。本書を最大限に活用して，教科書本文の理解を深めましょう。

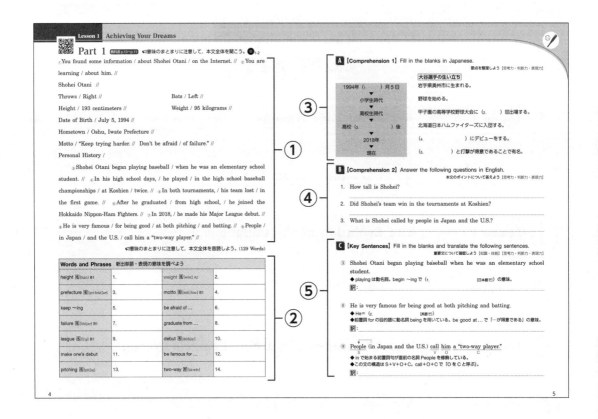

① 教科書本文

　意味のまとまりごとにスラッシュ（/）を入れました。ここで示した意味のまとまりを意識しながら音読しましょう。また学習がしやすいよう，一文ずつ番号を付けました。上部の二次元コードは本文音声のリスニングや音読に使用できる「スピーキング・トレーナー」にリンクしています。右ページに詳しい解説があります。

※本文中の グレーのマーカー は，教科書では印字されておらず，音声としてのみ配信している部分であることを示します。

※◯oは，生徒用音声CD（別売）のディスク番号とトラック番号を示します。

② Words and Phrases

　新出単語・表現の意味を調べて，意味を日本語で記入しましょう。単語の品詞と発音記号も示しました。A1～B2は，CEFR-Jでのレベルを示します。色の付いた単語は，読んで意味がわかるだけでなく，表現活動でも使えるようにしておきたい語です。

『CEFR-J Wordlist Version 1.6』東京外国語大学投野由紀夫研究室.
（URL: http://cefr-j.org/download.html より2021年2月ダウンロード）

③ **A** 問
━━

図表を日本語で完成させることで本文の理解を深める問題です。年表・地図・グラフなど，パートごとにさまざまな形の図表を完成させます。

④ **B** 問
━━

教科書本文に関連する英語の質問に対し，英語で答える問題です。教科書の **Q** とは別の問題としています。**A** 問で完成させた図表がヒントになる問題も含まれています。

⑤ **C** 問
━━

教科書の各文で，新出の文法事項や「Focus on Five Skill Areas」に関連したもの，また文構造が複雑なものや指示語を含むものなどを重要文と位置づけ，解説を加えました。解説を日本語や英語で完成させ，和訳をする問題です。

Web コンテンツ

スピーキング・トレーナー

本文の音声データ無料配信，音読用のボイスレコーダーが使用できます。

https://dg-w.jp/b/c6d0011

音声データ配信

・音声データを無料でダウンロード，または再生ができます。音声ファイルは MP3 形式，一括ダウンロードは ZIP 形式になっております。

　＊アップしてある音声データは著作権法で保護されています。音声データの利用は個人が私的に利用する場合に限られます。データを第三者に提供・販売することはできません。

ボイスレコーダー　アクセスキー：fhj66

・音読の学習効果をさらに高めるために，自分の発話の録音ができるボイスレコーダーを用意しました。PC やスマートフォンからご利用できます。

　ボイスレコーダーの使用にはユーザー ID とパスワードが必要です。ID とパスワードを自分で設定（半角英数字 5 文字以上）して，利用を開始してください。

メモ欄

ID	
パスワード	

＊ ID とパスワードは紛失しないようにしてください。万が一紛失した場合は，それまでに記録された学習履歴がすべて参照できなくなります。復元はできませんので，ご注意ください。

＊正常に動作しない場合は「ヘルプ」→「動作要件」をご確認ください。

Part 1　教科書 p.10〜p.11　🔊意味のまとまりに注意して，本文全体を聞こう。 ◉1-2

①You found some information / about Shohei Otani / on the Internet. // ②You are learning / about him. //

Shohei Otani //

Throws / Right //　　　　　　　　　　Bats / Left //

Height / 193 centimeters //　　　　　Weight / 95 kilograms //

Date of Birth / July 5, 1994 //

Hometown / Oshu, Iwate Prefecture //

Motto / "Keep trying harder. // Don't be afraid / of failure." //

Personal History /

　③Shohei Otani began playing baseball / when he was an elementary school student. // ④In his high school days, / he played / in the high school baseball championships / at Koshien / twice. // ⑤In both tournaments, / his team lost / in the first game. // ⑥After he graduated / from high school, / he joined the Hokkaido Nippon-Ham Fighters. // ⑦In 2018, / he made his Major League debut. // ⑧He is very famous / for being good / at both pitching / and batting. // ⑨People / in Japan / and the U.S. / call him a "two-way player." //

🔊意味のまとまりに注意して，本文全体を音読しよう。(129 Words)

Words and Phrases　新出単語・表現の意味を調べよう			
height 名[háɪt] B1	1.	weight 名[wéɪt] A2	2.
prefecture 名[príːfektʃər]	3.	motto 名[má(ː)toʊ] B1	4.
keep 〜ing	5.	be afraid of …	6.
failure 名[féɪljər] B1	7.	graduate from …	8.
league 名[líːg] B1	9.	debut 名[déɪbjuː]	10.
make one's debut	11.	be famous for …	12.
pitching 名[pítʃɪŋ]	13.	two-way 形[túːwéɪ]	14.

A 【Comprehension 1】 Fill in the blanks in Japanese.

要点を整理しよう【思考力・判断力・表現力】

大谷選手の生い立ち

1994年（1.　　　）月 5 日
▼
小学生時代
▼
高校生時代
▼
高校（3.　　　　　）後
▼
2018年
▼
現在

岩手県奥州市に生まれる。

野球を始める。

甲子園の高等学校野球大会に（2.　　　）回出場する。

北海道日本ハムファイターズに入団する。

（4.　　　　　　　　）にデビューをする。

（5.　　　　　）と打撃が得意であることで有名。

B 【Comprehension 2】 Answer the following questions in English.

本文のポイントについて答えよう【思考力・判断力・表現力】

1. How tall is Shohei?

   ....

2. Did Shohei's team win in the tournaments at Koshien?

   ....

3. What is Shohei called by people in Japan and the U.S.?

   ....

C 【Key Sentences】 Fill in the blanks and translate the following sentences.

重要文について確認しよう【知識・技能】【思考力・判断力・表現力】

③ Shohei Otani began playing baseball when he was an elementary school student.

◆ playing は動名詞。begin ～ing で（1.　　　　　　　　[日本語で]）の意味。

訳：...

⑧ He is very famous for being good at both pitching and batting.

◆ He ＝（2.　　　　　　　[英語で]）
◆前置詞 for の目的語に動名詞 being を用いている。be good at ... で「…が得意である」の意味。

訳：...

⑨ People (in Japan and the U.S.) call him a "two-way player."
　　　S　　　　　　　　　　　　　　 V　　O　　　　C

◆ in で始まる前置詞句が直前の名詞 People を修飾している。
◆この文の構造は S＋V＋O＋C。call＋O＋C で「O を C と呼ぶ」。

訳：...

Part 2 教科書 p.12 ◁意味のまとまりに注意して，本文全体を聞こう。 ◎1-4

①Shohei Otani always makes every effort / to achieve his dreams. // ②He gives us some useful hints / for achieving our own dreams. //

1 ③I am the youngest / of three children / in my family. // ④I was active / in my childhood, / and I liked sports / very much. // ⑤I enjoyed badminton / and swimming / before I started / to play baseball. //

2 ⑥My father was a member / of a nonprofessional baseball team, / and my older brother / also played baseball. // ⑦I joined a local baseball team / when I was seven years old. // ⑧This was the beginning / of my love / for baseball. //

3 ⑨My father was a coach / of my team, / so he taught me / how to practice. // ⑩He always told me / to learn the basics / of playing baseball. // ⑪Thanks to his advice, / I was able to become a better player. //

◁意味のまとまりに注意して，本文全体を音読しよう。(130 Words)

Words and Phrases 新出単語・表現の意味を調べよう			
make an effort	1.	achieve 動 [ətʃíːv] A2	2.
childhood 名 [tʃáɪldhʊ̀d] A2	3.	nonprofessional 形 [nà(ː)nprəféʃ(ə)n(ə)l] B2	4.
basic 名 [béɪsɪk] A2	5.	thanks to …	6.

A **【Comprehension 1】** Fill in the blanks in Japanese.

パラグラフごとの要点を整理しよう【思考力・判断力・表現力】

父親との野球の練習
チームのコーチをしていた父親が練習の方法を教えた。父親は野球の（5.　　　）を習得するように言った。

幼少期の大谷選手
（1.　　　）人兄弟の末っ子。スポーツが好きで，野球を始める前は（2.　　　　　　）や（3.　　　）が好きだった。

野球が好きになったきっかけ
父親や兄が野球をしていた。大谷選手は 7 歳のとき（4.　　　）に入部した。

B **【Comprehension 2】** Answer the following questions in English.

本文のポイントについて答えよう【思考力・判断力・表現力】

1. Does Shohei have any younger brothers?

2. What sport did Shohei's father play?

3. What made Shohei a better player?

C **【Key Sentences】** Fill in the blanks and translate the following sentences.

重要文について確認しよう【知識・技能】【思考力・判断力・表現力】

③ I am the youngest of three children in my family.
◆ I＝（1.　　　　[英語で]）。S＋V＋C の文である。
◆ youngest は形容詞 young の最上級。「of＋複数を表す名詞」で比較対象の範囲を示す。
訳：

⑤ I enjoyed badminton and swimming before I started to play baseball.
◆接続詞 before は，「…する前に」という意味で前後の節をつなぐ。
◆ start to ～で，（2.　　　　[日本語で]）。
訳：

⑨ My father was a coach of my team, so he taught me how to practice.
◆接続詞 so は「だから」という意味で，直前に述べたことの結果を述べる。
◆ teach＋O_1＋O_2 で「O_1 に O_2 を教える」。how to ～で「～する方法」。
訳：

Part 3 教科書 p.14 ◀意味のまとまりに注意して，本文全体を聞こう。 ◎1-6

④ ①In my high school days, / my coach, / Hiroshi Sasaki, / taught me a method / for achieving my goals and dreams. // ②The method was the use / of a "Target Achievement Sheet." // ③I believe / that it is very important / to decide on a goal / and make it clear. //

⑤ ④I will teach you / how to make a Target Achievement Sheet. // ⑤First, / divide a square / into nine equal parts. // ⑥Then, / write your final goal / in the central square. // ⑦In each square / around the central square, / set small targets / to achieve your final goal. // ⑧My final goal was / to become a professional baseball player / after high school. //

⑥ ⑨I learned the importance / of writing down goals / on paper. // ⑩Writing down your goals / can help you / as you try / to achieve them. //

◀意味のまとまりに注意して，本文全体を音読しよう。(124 Words)

Words and Phrases	新出単語・表現の意味を調べよう		
method 名 [méθəd] A2	1.	target 名 [tá:rɡət] A2	2.
achievement 名 [ətʃíːvmənt] B1	3.	sheet 名 [ʃíːt] B1	4.
decide on …	5.	divide 動 [dɪváɪd] A2	6.
divide A into B	7.	central 形 [séntr(ə)l] B1	8.

A 【Comprehension 1】 Fill in the blanks in Japanese.

パラグラフごとの要点を整理しよう【思考力・判断力・表現力】

高校時代にコーチに教わったこと
・(1.　　　　　　　　　　　) を使う という方法を教わった。

作り方
・図の A に (2.　　　　　　) を書き，B にそれを達成するための (3.　　　　　) を書き込む。大谷選手は A に「高校卒業後に (4.　　　　　) になる」と書いた。

B	B	B
B	A	B
B	B	B

目標を書き込むことの重要さ
・紙に目標を書き留めることの (5.　　　　　) を学んだ。

B 【Comprehension 2】 Answer the following questions in English.

本文のポイントについて答えよう【思考力・判断力・表現力】

1. Who taught Shohei a "Target Achievement Sheet"?

　..

2. What do you put in the squares around the central square?

　..

3. What can help you as you try to achieve your goals?

　..

C 【Key Sentences】 Fill in the blank and translate the following sentences.

重要文について確認しよう【知識・技能】【思考力・判断力・表現力】

③ It is very important <u>to decide on a goal and make it clear</u>.
形式主語　　　　　　　　　　　　　　　　・真主語
◆ It を形式主語として本来の主語の位置に置き，to-不定詞を真主語として後に置いている。
◆ make＋O＋C で（1.　　　　　　　　　 [日本語で]）の意味。
訳：..

⑦ In <u>each square</u> (around the central square), set small targets / to achieve your final goal.
◆ to-不定詞 to achieve … は副詞の働きをして，目的を表している。
訳：..

⑩ <u>Writing down your goals</u> can help you **as** you try to achieve them.
◆動名詞句 Writing down your goals がこの文の主語。
◆接続詞 as は「…するとき」という意味で前後の節をつなぐ。
訳：..

Part 4 教科書 p.16 意味のまとまりに注意して，本文全体を聞こう。 ◎1-8

7 ①What can you do / to achieve your dreams? // ②I have three important

things / to tell you. //

8 ③First, / you should ask yourself, / "What can I focus on / now?" // ④When I

hurt my leg / and couldn't pitch, / I focused / on batting. // ⑤As a result, / I made

remarkable progress / with my batting skills / during that period. //

9 ⑥Second, / you should understand / that failure can lead / to success. //

⑦Losing isn't the end. // ⑧You should change your frustration / into motivation. //

⑨I believe / that failure can become the basis / for success. //

10 ⑩Finally, / you should remember / that it is hard / to achieve big dreams. //

⑪You will need / to make every effort / and try hard / to achieve them. // ⑫Good

luck! //

意味のまとまりに注意して，本文全体を音読しよう。(111 Words)

Words and Phrases 新出単語・表現の意味を調べよう			
focus on …	1.	as a result	2.
remarkable 形 [rɪmáːrkəb(ə)l] B1	3.	progress 名 [prá(ː)grəs] B1	4.
make progress with …	5.	lead to …	6.
frustration 名 [frʌstréɪʃ(ə)n] B1	7.	motivation 名 [mòʊtəvéɪʃ(ə)n] B1	8.
change A into B	9.	basis 名 [béɪsɪs] B1	10.

A 【Comprehension 1】 Fill in the blanks in Japanese.

パラグラフごとの要点を整理しよう【思考力・判断力・表現力】

夢を実現するために大切なこと		
①今，自分は何に (1.　　　　　) できるかを自分自身に問いかけること（例：脚を故障して投球できないときに打撃練習をした結果，打撃の技術が高まった）。	②(2.　　　) は (3.　　　) につながることもあると理解すること。	③ (4.　　　　　) を実現することは困難であることだと覚えておくこと。

B 【Comprehension 2】 Answer the following questions in English.

本文のポイントについて答えよう【思考力・判断力・表現力】

1. What happened to Shohei while he focused on batting?

----

2. What can your frustration turn into?

----

3. Does Shohei think that achieving big dreams is easy?

C 【Key Sentences】 Fill in the blanks and translate the following sentences.

重要文について確認しよう【知識・技能】【思考力・判断力・表現力】

② I have three important things (to tell you).

◆ to tell ... は形容詞の働きをして，直前の three important things を修飾している。

訳：--

⑤ As a result, I made remarkable progress with my batting skills during that period.

◆ as a result は (1.　　　　　　[日本語で])，make progress with ... は
(2.　　　　　　[日本語で]) の意味。

訳：--

⑪ You will need to make every effort and try hard to achieve them.

◆ need to ～は「～する必要がある」という意味。

◆ them＝(3.　　　　　　[英語 2 語で])。

訳：--

Activity Plus 　教科書 p.20〜p.21　 ◁意味のまとまりに注意して，本文全体を聞こう。 ◎1-10

①You found some information / about young Japanese athletes / and a professional / on the Internet. // ②You are reading / about them / and listening / to them. //

③Young Japanese Athletes / and a Professional /

④Akane Yamaguchi / is a badminton player. // ⑤She was born / on June 6, 1997. // ⑥When she was in her third year / of junior high school, / she was selected / as the youngest member / of Japan's national badminton team. // ⑦In 2018, / she was ranked / first / in the world. // ⑧Her motto is / "Enjoy playing every game." //

⑨It is important / for you / to do better / than last year. // ⑩Great efforts are essential. //

⑪Mima Ito / is a table tennis player. // ⑫She was born / on October 21, 2000. // ⑬In 2018, / she won three gold medals / in Japan's national competition. // ⑭Her former partner / for doubles, / Miu Hirano, / is both her good friend / and good rival. //

⑮Thanks to my rivals, / I'm able to focus / on playing / now. // ⑯I want to thank my coaches, / rivals, / friends / and family / for supporting me / during my hardships. //

⑰Sota Fujii / is a professional *shogi* player. // ⑱He was born / on July 19, 2002. // ⑲On October 1, 2016, / he became a professional / when he was only 14 years old. // ⑳In 2018, / he got the seventh-dan / in *shogi*. //

㉑It is very important / for me / to keep finding the best way / to win. // ㉒The only way / to experience being a champion / is to become one, / so I always make every effort / to reach the top. //

◁意味のまとまりに注意して，本文全体を音読しよう。(236 Words)

Words and Phrases　新出単語・表現の意味を調べよう			
select 動 [səlékt] B2	1.	select A as B	2.
rank 動 [rǽŋk]	3.	essential 形 [ɪsénʃ(ə)l] B1	4.
medal 名 [méd(ə)l] A2	5.	competition 名 [kà(:)mpətíʃ(ə)n] A2	6.

former 形 [fɔ́ːrmər] B1	7.	rival 图 [ráɪv(ə)l] B2	8.
hardship 图 [háːrdʃìp] B1	9.		

A 【Comprehension 1】 Fill in the blanks in Japanese.

パラグラフごとの要点を整理しよう【思考力・判断力・表現力】

	山口茜選手 (バドミントン)	伊藤美誠選手 (卓球)	藤井聡太棋士 (将棋)
生年月日	1997年 (1.　　　) 月6日	2000年10月21日	2002年 (5.　　　) 月19日
戦績	2018年, 世界ランキング1位となる。	2018年, 日本の国内大会で3つの (3.　　　　) を獲得する。	2018年, 七段を獲得する。
大切だと考えていること	どの試合もプレーすることを (2.　　　　) こと。	(4.　　　　) のおかげで今, 競技に集中することができる。	(6.　　　　) ための最善の方法を見つけ続けることが重要だ。

B 【Comprehension 2】 Answer the following questions in English.

本文のポイントについて答えよう【思考力・判断力・表現力】

1. What is Akane's motto?

---

2. Who is Miu Hirano?

---

3. When did Sota become a professional?

C 【Key Sentences】 Fill in the blanks and translate the following sentences.

重要文について確認しよう【知識・技能】【思考力・判断力・表現力】

⑥ When she was in her third year of junior high school, she was selected as the youngest member of Japan's national badminton team.

◆ select A as B で (1.　　　　　[日本語で]) という意味。〈be-動詞＋過去分詞〉で受け身を表す。

訳：_____

㉒ The only way (to experience being a champion) is to become one, so I always
　 S　　　　　　　　　　　　　　　　　　V　　C
make every effort to reach the top.

◆ one＝a (2.　　　　　[英語で])。
◆ to experience ... は形容詞の働き, to reach ... は「〜するために」という副詞の働きをしている。

訳：_____

Part 1 教科書 p.26～p.27 ◁意味のまとまりに注意して，本文全体を聞こう。 ◉1-12

① You found a Q&A site / about the Japanese bento. //

② I'm planning to travel / to Japan / next week / and want to try some bentos. //

③ Any suggestions? //

④ Lilly //

⑤ You should visit / a Japanese convenience store. // ⑥ Each store has a large section / for bentos, / and you can choose one / from a wide variety. // ⑦ You can see / some typical Japanese foods, / such as sushi, / noodles / and curry. //

⑧ Victor //

⑨ You should try *ekiben*, / or "station bentos." // ⑩ You can buy them / at stations / for long-distance trains. // ⑪ Buy your bento before boarding / and enjoy it / on the train. // ⑫ At some stations, / you can buy popular local bentos, / such as a *gyutan* bento / at Sendai Station. //

⑬ Emily //

⑭ If you stay in a big city / like Tokyo or Osaka, / you should go to a business area / on your lunch break. // ⑮ A lot of restaurants sell bentos / to business people. // ⑯ They are made / by a restaurant chef, / but they are not so expensive. //

⑰ David //   ◁意味のまとまりに注意して，本文全体を音読しよう。(154 Words)

Words and Phrases	新出単語・表現の意味を調べよう		
Lilly [líli]	リリー	such as …	1.
Victor [víktər]	ヴィクター	variety 名 [vəráɪəti] B1	2.
typical 形 [típɪk(ə)l] B1	3.	Emily [ém(ə)li]	エミリー
long-distance 形 [lɔ̀ːŋdíst(ə)ns] B2	4.	David [déɪvɪd]	デイヴィッド

A 【**Comprehension 1**】 Fill in the blanks in Japanese.

要点を整理しよう【思考力・判断力・表現力】

人物	提案	理由
V Victor	(1.　　　　) に行くのがおすすめ	種類が多く，(2.　　　　) な日本の弁当を見ることもできる。
Emily	駅で (3.　　　　) を買うのがおすすめ	その地方で (4.　　　) の弁当を駅で買うことができる。
David	昼食時にビジネス街に行くのがおすすめ	レストランのシェフが作っているが (5.　　　) ではない。

B 【**Comprehension 2**】 Answer the following questions in English.

本文のポイントについて答えよう【思考力・判断力・表現力】

1. Why does Lilly want to know about Japanese bentos?

----

2. Who wrote that Lilly should try bentos made for business people?

----

3. If Lilly takes trains for a long-distance trip, what bentos should she try?

C 【**Key Sentences**】 Fill in the blanks and translate the following sentences.

重要文について確認しよう【知識・技能】【思考力・判断力・表現力】

③ Any suggestions?

◆ (1.　　　　　　　　 [英語 3 語で]) any suggestions? が省略された形の，くだけた表現である。

訳：--

⑦ You can see some typical Japanese foods, **such as** sushi, noodles and curry.

◆ such as ... は例を挙げるときに用いる。…には名詞が入る。

訳：--

⑭ If you stay in a big city **like** Tokyo or Osaka, you should go to a business area.

◆ If you ..., you should ～ 「もし…なら，～するほうがいい」。

◆ like ... は「…のような」の意味で，例を挙げるときに用いる。

訳：--

Part 2 教科書 p.28 ◁意味のまとまりに注意して，本文全体を聞こう。 ◎1-14

①The Japanese bento is growing popular overseas. // ②Many non-Japanese are enjoying making and eating bentos. // ③Why are they interested in this Japanese-style box lunch? //

1 ④"Do you want to take miso soup / with you for lunch? // ⑤Do you use a microwave?" // ⑥A French man is talking / to a young couple / in his Japanese lunchbox shop / in Kyoto. // ⑦He is one of the many foreign people / fascinated by Japanese bento culture. // ⑧He is selling Japanese lunchboxes / to travelers / in the shop. // ⑨He is also selling them / to people abroad / through the Internet. //

2 ⑩Many people in other countries / are surprised to know / that the Japanese bento is beautiful. // ⑪In a typical bento, / a variety of bite-sized foods / are neatly arranged / into a lunchbox. // ⑫It is very colorful / and looks like a work of art. // ⑬More and more people / want to try making this art. //

3 ⑭In addition, / the bento is healthy. // ⑮It usually contains many foods, / like rice, / meat, / fish, / vegetables / and fruit. // ⑯It is a full-course meal / in a small box. //　　　◁意味のまとまりに注意して，本文全体を音読しよう。(168 Words)

Words and Phrases 新出単語・表現の意味を調べよう			
non-Japanese 图 [n(à):ndʒæpəníːz]	1.	microwave 图 [máɪkrəwèɪv] B2	2.
couple 图 [kʌ́p(ə)l] A2	3.	lunchbox 图 [lʌ́n(t)ʃbà(ː)ks]	4.
fascinate 動 [fǽsɪnèɪt] B1	5.	a variety of …	6.
bite-sized 形 [báɪtsàɪzd]	7.	neatly 副 [níːtli]	8.
arrange 動 [əréɪn(d)ʒ] B1	9.	look like …	10.
more and more …	11.	in addition	12.
contain 動 [kəntéɪn] B1	13.	full-course 形 [fúlkɔ̀ːrs]	14.

A 【Comprehension 1】 Fill in the blanks in Japanese.

日本の（1.　　　　　）文化が海外の多くの人を魅了している。

そのうちの1人であるフランス人男性
・旅行者に日本の弁当箱を販売している。
・（2.　　　　　）での販売もしている。

・日本の弁当は（3.　　　　　）ことに驚かされる。一口サイズで，きちんと弁当箱に詰められ，色鮮やかで芸術作品のようだ。
・日本の弁当は（4.　　　　　）だ。多くの食べ物が含まれ，フルコースの食事になっている。

B 【Comprehension 2】 Answer the following questions in English.

1. What kind of shop does the French man own in Kyoto?

　　..

2. In a typical bento, what is neatly arranged into a lunchbox?

　　..

3. What are examples of foods contained in a lunchbox?

　　..

C 【Key Sentences】 Fill in the blanks and translate the following sentences.

④ Do you want to **take** miso soup **with** you for lunch?

　◆take ... with＋人「…を持っていく」。with＋人は特に訳す必要がないことが多い。
　◆音読するときは，英語のリズムに注意して読む。また Yes-No 疑問文はふつう上昇調で読む。
　訳：..

⑦ He is one of the many foreign people (**fascinated** by Japanese bento culture).

　◆過去分詞の形容詞用法。fascinated by ... は前にある people を修飾。fascinate は「（1.　　　　　
　　[日本語で]）」の意味の他動詞で，people は魅了されるという関係にあるため，過去分詞を用いている。
　◆ one of ...「…のうちの1つ［1人］」。…にはふつう複数形の名詞が入る。
　訳：..

⑬ More and more people want to **try making** this art.

　◆ this art は（2.　　　　　 [日本語で]）のこと。
　◆ try 〜ing は「（試しに）〜してみる」の意味。
　訳：..

Part 3 教科書 p.29 ◀意味のまとまりに注意して，本文全体を聞こう。 ◎1-16

④ ①The idea of bringing bentos / to school or work / is not unique / to Japan. //

⑤ ②Dutch people prepare lunches / of simple ham or cheese sandwiches, / along with some fruit, / like an apple or a banana. // ③They make sandwiches / for themselves, / and it is not common / to prepare them / for someone else. //

⑥ ④American people put sandwiches, / fruit, / a small carton of juice, / and sometimes snacks / into a lunchbox. // ⑤There are a variety of sandwiches, / but peanut butter and jelly sandwiches / have been popular / among children / for a long time. //

⑦ ⑥The Chinese-style box lunch / contains rice / covered with one or two main dishes, / such as stir-fried vegetables. // ⑦Chinese people use containers / to carry bentos, / and they always warm the box lunch up / before they eat it. // ⑧This is because they don't like to eat cold food. //

◀意味のまとまりに注意して，本文全体を音読しよう。 (133 Words)

Words and Phrases	新出単語・表現の意味を調べよう		
unique 形[juːníːk] B1	1.	be unique to …	2.
Dutch 形[dʌtʃ]	3.	along with …	4.
carton 图[káːrt(ə)n] B1	5.	peanut 图[píːnʌt] B1	6.
jelly 图[dʒéli] A2	7.	for a long time	8.
be covered with …	9.	stir-fried 形[stəːrfráid]	10.
container 图 [kəntéɪnər] A2	11.	this is because …	12.

A 【Comprehension 1】 Fill in the blanks in Japanese.

① (1.　　　　[国名])
・ハムとチーズのサンドイッチ　　　・果物
・(2.　　　　) のために作る。
②アメリカ
・サンドイッチ，果物，ジュースを
(3.　　　　) に入れる。
・ピーナッツバターやゼリーのサンドイッチも人気。

③中国
・炒めた野菜など主菜をかぶせた (4.　　　　) を容器に入れる。
・容器を使用し，(5.　　　　) から食べる。

B 【Comprehension 2】 Answer the following questions in English.

本文のポイントについて答えよう【思考力・判断力・表現力】

1. Which is common for Dutch people, making sandwiches for themselves or preparing them for someone else?

----

2. What kind of sandwich has been popular in America?

----

3. Why do Chinese people use containers for lunchbox?

C 【Key Sentences】 Fill in the blank and translate the following sentences.

重要文について確認しよう【知識・技能】【思考力・判断力・表現力】

① The idea of bringing bentos to school or work is not unique to Japan.
　　　　　　　　　　　　　　　　　　　　　　　S　　　　　V　　　C
◆ the idea of ～ing 「～するという考え」。of は idea の内容を説明する「同格」の用法。
◆ be unique to ... は「…に特有である」の意味。
訳 : --

⑤ Peanut butter and jelly sandwiches **have been** popular among children for a long time.
◆現在完了形 have been は「ずっと…である」という継続の意味。
◆ among ... は「…の間で」の意味。…には3人以上の「もの・人」が入ることが多い。
訳 : --

⑧ **This is because** they don't like to eat cold food.
◆ this is because ... は「これは…だからである」の意味。
◆ This は前の文の内容を指す。(1.　　　　　　　　　　[日本語で]) ということ。
訳 : --

Part 4 教科書 p.32 ◁意味のまとまりに注意して，本文全体を聞こう。◉1-18

⑧ ①Japanese homemade bentos are full of love. // ②In Japan, / many high school students eat a bento / made by their parents / for lunch. // ③The parents get up early / in the morning / and make their bentos. // ④"Will my son like these side dishes?" // ⑤"Is this bento well-balanced for my daughter?" // ⑥They always think about such things / while they are making bentos. //

⑨ ⑦*Kyaraben*, / or "character bentos," / are created from parents' love. // ⑧They want to make the food attractive / and encourage their kids / to eat properly. // ⑨Their kids are able to eat / even their least favorite foods. //

⑩ ⑩Japanese parents put messages / into the bentos, / and the children receive them. // ⑪Some people in other countries / have noticed this function of bentos, / and they also enjoy making them. // ⑫Japanese-style bentos / can be a remarkable communication tool / around the world. //

◁意味のまとまりに注意して，本文全体を音読しよう。(133 Words)

Words and Phrases 新出単語・表現の意味を調べよう			
homemade 形 [hóʊmmèɪd]	1.	well-balanced 形 [wèlbǽlənst] B2	2.
attractive 形 [ətrǽktɪv] A2	3.	encourage ... to ～	4.
properly 副 [prá(:)pərli] B1	5.	function 名 [fʌ́ŋ(k)ʃ(ə)n] A2	6.

A 【Comprehension 1】 Fill in the blanks in Japanese.

パラグラフごとの要点を整理しよう【思考力・判断力・表現力】

> **高校生のお弁当は？**
> ・日本の手作り弁当には愛情が込められている。
> ・(1.　　　　) が朝早く起きて，弁当を作る。

> **手作り弁当の例①**
> 食べ物を (2.　　　　) にして，子供たちがきらいな食べ物でもきちんと食べられるように工夫している。

> **手作り弁当の例②**
> 弁当に（3.　　　　) を入れて，子供たちはそれを受け取る。日本スタイルの弁当はコミュニケーションの道具になる。

B 【Comprehension 2】 Answer the following questions in English.

本文のポイントについて答えよう【思考力・判断力・表現力】

1. What are Japanese homemade bentos full of?

   ----

2. How can parents encourage their children to eat their least favorite foods?

   ----

3. When the children eat bentos made by their parents, what do they receive?

C 【Key Sentences】 Translate the following sentences.

重要文について確認しよう【知識・技能】【思考力・判断力・表現力】

② Many high school students eat a bento (**made** by their parents) for lunch.
   ◆分詞の形容詞用法 made ... は前の a bento を修飾する。
   訳：--

⑧ They want to make the food attractive and **encourage** their kids **to** eat properly.
   　　　　　　　　V　　O　　　C
   ◆ make＋O＋C で「O を C にする」の意味。
   ◆ encourage＋O＋to ～で「O に～するように促す [仕向ける]」の意味。
   訳：--

⑪ Some people in other countries **have noticed** this function of bentos.
   ◆現在完了形 have noticed は「…に気づいている」という完了の意味。過去に見聞きして，現在も知っていることを表す。
   訳：--

Activity Plus 教科書 p.36～p.37 🔊意味のまとまりに注意して，本文全体を聞こう。 ◎1-20

①You are interested / in joining a bento contest. // ②You are looking at a leaflet / about it. //

③International Bento Contest 2025 //

④The White Snow Bento Company / has held an International Bento Contest / since 2016. // ⑤The 10th contest will start / on April 25, / 2025. // ⑥The theme this year is / "a bento using locally-produced foods." // ⑦The first-prize winner / will get a pair of round-trip tickets / to Hokkaido / from his/her country. // ⑧We hope / that you will take part in this contest! //

⑨Contest Rules //

⑩Entry Period: / From April 25 / to May 6, / 2025 //

⑪Theme // A bento / using locally-produced foods //

⑫How to Enter // Fill out the entry form, / and submit your recipe and pictures / through the contest website. //

・⑬Take two pictures. // ⑭One should be a picture / of all foods before cooking, / and the other should be a picture / of the completed bento. //

⑮Entry Conditions // You must be 15 or older / to join the contest. //

⑯For more information, / visit our website / at https://www.wsbc.com/2025/contest/ //

🔊意味のまとまりに注意して，本文全体を音読しよう。(163 Words)

Words and Phrases 新出単語・表現の意味を調べよう			
leaflet 名[líːflət] B2	1.	theme 名[θíːm] B2	2.
locally 副[lóuk(ə)li]	3.	a pair of …	4.
round-trip 形[ràundtríp]	5.	take part in …	6.
fill out …	7.	entry 名[éntri] B1	8.
submit 動[səbmít] B2	9.	one …, the other ～	10.
complete 動[kəmplíːt] B1	11.		

A 【Comprehension 1】 Fill in the blanks in Japanese.

要点を整理しよう【思考力・判断力・表現力】

2025年　第10回　弁当コンテスト	
今年度の テーマ	(1.　　　　　　　) を使った弁当
エントリー 期間	2025年4月25日〜 (2.　　　　　) 月6日
応募方法	応募用紙に記入し，(3.　　　　) と写真を提出してください。なお，写真は2枚（調理する前と完成後）を提出してください。
参加基準	(4.　　　) 歳以上
賞	最優秀賞：(5.　　　) への往復ペアチケット

B 【Comprehension 2】 Answer the following questions in English.

本文のポイントについて答えよう【思考力・判断力・表現力】

1. What do you get if you win first prize?

   ----

2. What photos do you have to submit to enter this contest?

   ----

3. When does this contest start?

C 【Key Sentences】 Fill in the blank and translate the following sentences.

重要文について確認しよう【知識・技能】【思考力・判断力・表現力】

④ The White Snow Bento Company **has held** an International Bento Contest since 2016.

◆現在完了形 has held は「(…以来ずっと) 開催している」という継続の意味。

訳： ---

⑥ The theme this year is "a bento (**using** locally-produced foods)."

◆現在分詞の形容詞用法で，using ... はすぐ前の a bento を修飾している。分詞1語で修飾する場合はふつう名詞の前に置かれる。

訳： ---

⑭ **One** should be a picture of all foods before cooking, **and the other** should be a picture of the completed bento.

◆ One ..., and the other 〜は「1つは…で，もう1つは〜」の意味。

◆ completed は直後の bento を修飾し，completed bento で「(1.　　　　[日本語で])」の意味。

訳： ---

Part 1 教科書 p.42〜p.43 ◁意味のまとまりに注意して，本文全体を聞こう。 ◎1-22

①You want to learn some information / about cellphones and public phones. //

②You are listening to a presentation / about them. //

③The total numbers of cellphones and public phones / in Japan / from 1990 to 2017 //

④The graph shows the changes / in the total numbers / of cellphones and public phones / in Japan / from 1990 to 2017. //

⑤As you can see, / before 1993, / cellphones were not very common. //

⑥From 1999 to 2008, / the total number of cellphones increased / by more than 100%. // ⑦In 2011, / there were more than 120 million cellphones. // ⑧This means / that the number of cellphones / was greater / than the population / of Japan. // ⑨Even today, / the number is increasing / year by year. //

⑩On the other hand, / from 1990 to 2017, / the number of public phones decreased / by more than 80%. // ⑪Will the number of public phones / continue to decrease / year by year? //

◁意味のまとまりに注意して，本文全体を音読しよう。(140 Words)

Words and Phrases	新出単語・表現の意味を調べよう		
the number of …	1.	as you see	2.
population 图 [pὰ(:)pjəléɪʃ(ə)n] A2	3.	year by year	4.
on the other hand	5.	decrease 動 [dɪkríːs] B1	6.

A 【**Comprehension 1**】 Fill in the blanks in Japanese.

要点を整理しよう【思考力・判断力・表現力】

グラフは日本での1990年〜2017年の　（1.　　　　　　）　と　（2.　　　　　　　）　の合計台数を示す。

携帯電話の台数
1999年から2008年の間に
（3.　　　　）　倍以上になった。

公衆電話の台数
1990年から2017年の間に，
（4.　　　　）　% 以上減少した。

B 【**Comprehension 2**】 Answer the following questions in English.

本文のポイントについて答えよう【思考力・判断力・表現力】

1. What does the red bar show?

   ....

2. Which is larger, the number of cellphones or that of Japanese people?

   ....

3. From 1990 to 2017, what percentage did the number of public phones decrease by?

   ....

C 【**Key Sentences**】 Fill in the blanks and translate the following sentences.

重要文について確認しよう【知識・技能】【思考力・判断力・表現力】

⑥ The total number of cellphones increased by more than 100%.

◆ the total number of ... で「(1.　　　　　　[日本語で])」の意味。

◆ increase by more than 100% の by は「差異」を表す。

訳 : ....

⑧ This means that the number of cellphones was greater than the population
   　　　　　　　　　　　　　S　　　　　　　V　　C
   of Japan.

◆ This の内容は「(2.　　　　　　　　　　　[日本語で])」ということ。

◆ the number of cellphones は単数扱い。be-動詞は was となることに注意。

訳 : ....

⑪ Will the number of public phones **continue to** decrease year by year?
   　　　　　　　　S

◆主語は the number of public phones。助動詞 will が文頭に出て疑問文になっている。

◆ continue to 〜「〜し続ける」。continue の後は to-不定詞も動名詞も入る。

訳 : ....

Part 2 教科書 p.44 ◁意味のまとまりに注意して，本文全体を聞こう。 ◎1-24

①Can you live / without your cellphone? // ②Most people use their cellphones / for various purposes. // ③The evolution of the cellphone / over the last 50 years / is an amazing story. //

1 ④A lot of things have happened / in the last 50 years. // ⑤When it comes to technology, / "50 years ago" / is like ancient times. // ⑥What has evolved / surprisingly fast / as technology has developed? // ⑦Yes, / it's the cellphone. //

2 ⑧Nowadays, / seven billion cellphones are used / around the world. // ⑨Who invented the cellphone? // ⑩It was Dr. Martin Cooper, / an engineer / at a telecommunications company / in the U.S. //

3 ⑪Cooper invented the first cellphone / in 1973. // ⑫He wanted to make a phone / which people could carry / with them anywhere. // ⑬The first model / was 22.5 centimeters long / and weighed about one kilogram. // ⑭The battery lasted / only 20 minutes. //

4 ⑮In 1973, / Cooper stood on a street / in New York / and made a phone call. // ⑯He said, / "I'm calling / from a cellphone! // ⑰A real handheld, / portable cellphone!" //

◁意味のまとまりに注意して，本文全体を音読しよう。(156 Words)

Words and Phrases 新出単語・表現の意味を調べよう			
evolution 名 [èvəlúːʃ(ə)n] B2	1.	when it comes to …	2.
evolve 動 [ɪvá(ː)lv] B2	3.	nowadays 副 [náʊədèɪz] A2	4.
Martin Cooper [máːrt(ə)n kúːpər]	マーチン・クーパー	telecommunication 名 [tèləkəmjùːnɪkéɪʃ(ə)n] B1	5.
weigh 動 [wéɪ] A2	6.	battery 名 [bǽt(ə)ri] A2	7.
make a (phone) call	8.	handheld 形 [hǽndhèld]	9.
portable 形 [pɔ́ːrtəb(ə)l]	10.		

26

A【**Comprehension 1**】Fill in the blanks in Japanese.

パラグラフごとの要点を整理しよう【思考力・判断力・表現力】

テクノロジーの発展	
50年前は一昔。最も進化を遂げたテクノロジーの産物の一つに（₁.　　　　　　　　　）がある。	
携帯電話の発明	
だれ	マーチン・クーパー。⇒アメリカの（₂.　　　　）会社の技術者。
クーパーが初めて発明した携帯電話	
特徴	どこにでも持ち運びができる。 全長：（₃.　　　　）センチ。重量：約（₄.　　　　）キロ。
携帯電話の実用に成功。 （₅.　　　　　　　）の通りで，クーパー自身がその電話を利用した。	

B【**Comprehension 2**】Answer the following questions in English.

本文のポイントについて答えよう【思考力・判断力・表現力】

1. What kind of phone did Cooper want to invent?

   ----

2. How long did the battery of the first cellphone model last?

   ----

3. In 1973, where did Cooper make a phone call?

C【**Key Sentences**】Fill in the blanks and translate the following sentences.

重要文について確認しよう【知識・技能】【思考力・判断力・表現力】

⑤ When it comes to technology, "50 years ago" is like ancient times.
　　　　　　　　　　　　　　　　　　　S　　　　　V　　　C
　◆it は特定のものを指すわけではない。when it comes to ... で「（₁.　　　　[日本語で]）」
　　の意味。
　◆引用符の中の50 years ago が主語となっている。
　訳：--

⑩ It was Dr. Martin Cooper, / an engineer / at a telecommunications company /
　in the U.S.
　◆Dr. Martin Cooper と an engineer は同格の関係。意味のまとまりに注意して読む。
　訳：--

⑫ He wanted to make a phone (**which** people could carry with them anywhere).
　◆関係代名詞 which を含む節が，先行詞 a phone を修飾する。
　◆He＝（₂.　　　　[英語で]），them＝（₃.　　　　[英語で]）。
　訳：--

Part 3 教科書p.45 ◀意味のまとまりに注意して，本文全体を聞こう。◉1-26

5 ①The first cellphone / for public use / was released / on the market / in 1983. // ②It was only for talking. // ③Its screen was so small / that it was not easy / to use the cellphone. // ④Since then, / telecommunications companies / have put their efforts / into adding other functions, / along with the talking function. //

6 ⑤In 2000, / a camera function was added / to cellphones. // ⑥The quality of the images was low, / so people at that time / thought of it / as an extra. // ⑦Then, / "the wallet cellphone" was introduced / in 2004. // ⑧Thanks to it, / people could buy things / with their cellphones. // ⑨As various features were added, / screens became bigger / and cellphones became easier to use. // ⑩People came to use cellphones / instead of other devices, / such as dictionaries and music players. //

7 ⑪Cellphones are not just for talking anymore. // ⑫They are portable devices. // ⑬Companies have developed various applications / and have changed cellphones / into toolboxes / with a solution / for almost every need. //

◀意味のまとまりに注意して，本文全体を音読しよう。(152 Words)

Words and Phrases	新出単語・表現の意味を調べよう		
release 動[rɪlíːs] A2	1.	so … that 〜	2.
add A to B	3.	quality 名[kwá(ː)ləti] A2	4.
at that time	5.	think of A as B	6.
extra 名[ékstrə] A2	7.	wallet 名[wá(ː)lət] A2	8.
feature 名[fíːtʃər] A2	9.	come to 〜	10.
instead of …	11.	device 名[dɪváɪs] B1	12.
application 名 [æplɪkéɪʃ(ə)n] B1	13.	toolbox 名[túːlbà(ː)ks]	14.
solution 名[səlúːʃ(ə)n] A2	15.		

A 【Comprehension 1】 Fill in the blanks in Japanese.

パラグラフごとの要点を整理しよう【思考力・判断力・表現力】

一般利用向けの携帯電話機能	
1983年	(1.　　　　) 機能しかなかった。
▼ 2000年	(2.　　　　) 機能
▼ 2004年〜	(3.　　　　) 機能 その他追加された機能の例（4.　　　　），（5.　　　　）
▼ 現在	持ち運べる機器としてさまざまな（6.　　　　）が開発される。

B 【Comprehension 2】 Answer the following questions in English.

本文のポイントについて答えよう【思考力・判断力・表現力】

1. When was the first cellphone for public use released on the market?

---

2. When a camera function was added to the cellphones, why did people think of it as an extra?

---

3. What have companies developed to meet people's needs?

C 【Key Sentences】 Fill in the blank and translate the following sentences.

重要文について確認しよう【知識・技能】【思考力・判断力・表現力】

③ Its screen was so small that it <u>was</u> not <u>easy</u> to use the cellphone.
　　　　　　　　　　　　　　　　　　V　　　　C

◆ that-節内の it は形式主語で，真主語は（1.　　　　　[英語4語で]）

訳：-----

⑨ **As** various features were added, screens became bigger and cellphones became easier to use.

◆ as は「…するにつれて」の意味。
◆ become＋比較級は「より…になる」の意味。

訳：-----

⑬ Companies have **changed** cellphones **into** toolboxes with a solution for almost every need.

◆ change A into B で「AをBへと変える」の意味。

訳：-----

29

Part 4 教科書 p.48 ◀意味のまとまりに注意して，本文全体を聞こう。 ◎1-28

⑧ ①Smartphones were introduced / in 2007. // ②Today, / most people have a smartphone. // ③Some people expect / that smartphones will eventually take over the cellphone market. //

⑨ ④The cellphone has been evolving rapidly / in the past decade. // ⑤Both its appearance and purpose / have changed / during that time. // ⑥People need more functions / on their cellphones, / and companies are trying / to meet their needs. // ⑦The evolution of the cellphone / is an important event / in the history / of telecommunications technology. //

⑩ ⑧In the future, / cellphones will go through / another big change. // ⑨It is expected / that we will not need / a physical screen / at all / in the near future. // ⑩It is thought / that we will be able to link the devices / to our brain / and control them / with our thoughts. // ⑪This will be a technologically-assisted form / of telepathy. //

⑪ ⑫What do you think / the future phone will look like? // ⑬You may wonder, / "How will we change the cellphone?" // ⑭The real question is, / "How will the cellphone change us?" // ◀意味のまとまりに注意して，本文全体を音読しよう。(158 Words)

Words and Phrases 新出単語・表現の意味を調べよう			
expect 動[ɪkspékt] A2	1.	eventually 副 [ɪvén(t)ʃu(ə)li] B1	2.
take over …	3.	rapidly 副 [rǽpɪdli] B1	4.
decade 名[dékeɪd] B2	5.	appearance 名 [əpíər(ə)ns] A2	6.
go through …	7.	not … at all	8.
physical 形[fízɪk(ə)l] A2	9.	link 動 [líŋk] B1	10.
link A to B	11.	technologically 副 [tèknəlá(:)dʒɪk(ə)li]	12.
assist 動 [əsíst] B1	13.	telepathy 名 [təlépəθi]	14.

A 【**Comprehension 1**】 Fill in the blanks in Japanese.

パラグラフごとの要点を整理しよう【思考力・判断力・表現力】

(1.　　　　) 年 ▼ (現在から) 過去10年間	スマートフォンの登場
	スマートフォンの急速な進化 (2.　　　　) と用途が変化
未来	もう一つの大きな変化を迎える ⇩ (3.　　　　) な画面がなくなり, (4.　　　　) と結び付けて思考で操作できる。

B 【**Comprehension 2**】 Answer the following questions in English.

本文のポイントについて答えよう【思考力・判断力・表現力】

1. What will be the main item in the cellphone market?

　---

2. What do people need on their cellphones?

　---

3. In the future, what will we be able to link the devices to?

C 【**Key Sentences**】 Fill in the blanks and translate the following sentences.

重要文について確認しよう【知識・技能】【思考力・判断力・表現力】

③ Some people **expect that** smartphones will eventually take over the cellphone market.

　◆ expect＋that-節「…ということを期待する」。that-節の主語は (1.　　　　　　　 [英語で])。

　訳:---

④ The cellphone **has been evolving** rapidly in the past decade.

　◆ have been ～ing は現在完了進行形で，動作が進行し継続している状態を表す。「(ずっと) ～し続けている」。

　◆ in the past decade は「過去10年間に」の意味。

　訳:---

⑩ **It** is thought **that** we will be able to link the devices to our brain and control them with our thoughts.

　◆ It is thought that ... 「…と考えられている」。

　◆ them＝(2.　　　　　　 [英語で])。

　訳:---

Activity Plus 　教科書 p.52～p.53 　🔊意味のまとまりに注意して，本文全体を聞こう。　◉1-30

①Koji and Airi are making a presentation / about their ideas / for a future phone. //

②"A Special Contact Lens" //

③Hi. // ④I'm Koji. // ⑤My idea for a future phone / is a lens type of phone. // ⑥I named it / "A Special Contact Lens." //

⑦You can wear a lens / in your eye / like a normal contact lens. // ⑧The lens can catch / your brain waves. // ⑨When it is necessary, / a screen automatically appears / in the air. // ⑩Only the user / can see it. // ⑪The phone combines / several computers / through the Internet. // ⑫You can operate it / with your thoughts. //

⑬"New Face: Part of My Fashion" //

⑭Hi. // ⑮I'm Airi. // ⑯Today, / I'm going to tell you / about my idea / for a future phone. // ⑰I call it "New Face." // ⑱It's part of my fashion. //

⑲The phone is / an earring and a bracelet. // ⑳The earring shows the screen / in front of you. // ㉑The bracelet is a Wi-Fi hub. // ㉒It connects / to the Internet. //

㉓It's a cool future phone! //

🔊意味のまとまりに注意して，本文全体を音読しよう。(157 Words)

Words and Phrases　新出単語・表現の意味を調べよう			
make a presentation	1.	contact 名[ká(:)ntækt] A2	2.
lens 名[lénz]	3.	normal 形[nɔ́ːrm(ə)l] A2	4.
automatically 副 [ɔ̀ːtəmǽtɪk(ə)li] A2	5.	combine 動[kəmbáɪn] B1	6.
operate 動[á(:)pərèɪt] A2	7.	part of …	8.
earring 名[íərɪ̀ŋ] A2	9.	in front of …	10.
bracelet 名[bréɪslət] B1	11.	Wi-Fi 名[wáɪfàɪ]	ワイファイ
hub 名[hʌ́b]	12.		

A【**Comprehension 1**】Fill in the blanks in Japanese.

> コウジのアイディア
> 形状：コンタクトレンズ
>
> 目に装着し，（1.　　　　）をとらえることで動く。画面は（2.　　　　）に現れ，自分の（3.　　　　）で操作する。

> アイリのアイディア
> 形状：アクセサリー
>
> イヤリングで（4.　　　　）を映し，ブレスレットは（5.　　　　）の役割を果たす。

B【**Comprehension 2**】Answer the following questions in English.

1. What does Koji's future phone look like?

　　--

2. How can we operate "A Special Contact Lens"?

　　--

3. What is the role of the bracelet of "New Face"?

　　--

C【**Key Sentences**】Fill in the blank and translate the following sentences.

⑥ I named it "A Special Contact Lens."
　S　V　O　　　　C
　◆ it が O，A Special Contact Lens が C の S＋V＋O＋C の文型。
　◆ it＝a (1.　　　　　　　　[英語 2 語で])
　訳：--

⑨ When it is necessary, a screen automatically appears in the air.
　◆ When it is necessary「必要なときは」。
　訳：--

⑯ Today, I'm going to tell you about my idea for a future phone.
　◆ Today, I'm going to tell you about … は，プレゼンテーションなどで話題を切り出すときに使う表現。
　訳：--

Part 1 教科書 p.58~p.59 ◁意味のまとまりに注意して，本文全体を聞こう。 ◎ 1-32

① You are visiting a zoo. // ② You see giant pandas / and find a notice / in front of their cage. // ③ Also, / you hear an announcement / about pandas. //

④ Giant Pandas //

⑤ Height: / Adults can grow / to more than 120 centimeters //

⑥ Weight: / 100-150 kilograms /

⑦ A baby panda is / about 1/900 the size / of its mother. //

⑧ Population: / About 1,800 / in the wild / (about 400 in zoos) //

⑨ Habitat: / Bamboo forests / in China //

⑩ Pandas first came to Ueno Zoo / from China / in 1972 / as a symbol of the friendship / between China and Japan. // ⑪ A lot of people / went to see them / at the zoo. // ⑫ In 1994, / a panda came to Wakayama. // ⑬ There is a research base there / for giant pandas. // ⑭ More than ten pandas / have been born there. // ⑮ Pandas are very popular / all over Japan. //

⑯ This animal / with a black and white coat / is loved / around the world. // ⑰ Pandas live mainly in bamboo forests / in China. // ⑱ They must eat / from 10 to 40 kilograms / of bamboo / every day, / and they need 4,000 kilocalories / a day / to stay alive. // ⑲ In order to save energy, / they try not to move much. // ⑳ They seem to move / very slowly, / but pandas are very good at climbing trees. //

㉑ The panda is special / for World Wide Fund for Nature, / or WWF. // ㉒ It has been WWF's symbol / since its foundation / in 1961. // ㉓ Since then, / the number of pandas / has increased / little by little. // ㉔ They are symbols / of all endangered species. //　　◁意味のまとまりに注意して，本文全体を音読しよう。(235 Words)

Words and Phrases 新出単語・表現の意味を調べよう			
announcement 名 [ənáʊnsmənt] B1	1.	habitat 名 [hǽbɪtæt] B1	2.
all over …	3.	kilocalorie 名 [kíləkæləri]	4.

in order to ～	5.	seem 動 [síːm] A2	6.
fund 名 [fʌ́nd] B1	7.	foundation 名 [faʊndéɪʃ(ə)n] B1	8.
little by little	9.	endangered 形 [ɪndéɪn(d)ʒərd] A2	10.
species 名 [spíːʃiːz] B2	11.		

A 【Comprehension 1】 Fill in the blanks in Japanese.

要点を整理しよう【思考力・判断力・表現力】

日本におけるパンダ	パンダの習性	WWF とパンダ
・1972年に（1.　　　）から上野動物園にやってくる。 ・1994年に和歌山にやってきて，そこで（2.　　　）頭以上が生まれている。	・主な生息地 　中国の（3.　　　）。 ・1日の食事 　10～40キログラムの（4.　　　）。 ・活動 　（5.　　　）を節約するため，あまり動かない。	・1961年の（6.　　　）以来，パンダが WWF のシンボルマークになっている。

B 【Comprehension 2】 Answer the following questions in English.

本文のポイントについて答えよう【思考力・判断力・表現力】

1. How many giant pandas are there in the wild?

　

2. What can pandas do very well?

　

C 【Key Sentences】 Fill in the blanks and translate the following sentences.

重要文について確認しよう【知識・技能】【思考力・判断力・表現力】

⑭ More than ten pandas **have been** born there.

◆現在完了形は完了の用法。過去から現在までのことを述べている。

◆ there＝at a research （1.　　　　　[英語で]）。

訳：

⑲ In order to save energy, they try **not to** move much.

◆ in order to ～は （2.　　　　　[日本語で]）という意味。not を to-不定詞の直前に置くと，to-不定詞の意味を否定する。

訳：

Part 2　教科書 p.60　◁意味のまとまりに注意して，本文全体を聞こう。　◎1-34

①Almost everyone / likes to see pandas. // ②But how about snakes? // ③Are they necessary / for our planet, / or not? //

① ④What do pandas, / polar bears / and gorillas / have in common? // ⑤Yes, / they are all animals. // ⑥In addition to being animals, / they are all endangered animals. // ⑦They might disappear / in the near future. // ⑧Climate change, / pollution / and human activities / are threatening their survival. //

② ⑨The International Union for the Conservation of Nature, / or IUCN, / is working / to save species / from extinction. // ⑩The IUCN Red List of Threatened Species / is used / to guide decision-making / for conservation action. // ⑪According to the list, / more than 13,000 animal species / are threatened / with extinction. //

③ ⑫We all care about / saving species / from extinction, / but a question might come to mind: / "Why should endangered species be protected?" // ⑬It is because all species play a role / in nature. // ⑭All species of life / on earth / are connected to each other / and are needed / for our planet / to stay healthy. // ⑮All animals are part of the global ecosystem / and are necessary / for the balance / of nature. //

◁意味のまとまりに注意して，本文全体を音読しよう。(172 Words)

Words and Phrases　新出単語・表現の意味を調べよう			
polar 形 [póulər] B2	1.	have … in common	2.
in addition to …	3.	climate 名 [kláimət] B1	4.
threaten 動 [θrét(ə)n] B2	5.	survival 名 [sərváɪv(ə)l] B1	6.
union 名 [júːnjən] B1	7.	conservation 名 [kà(:)nsərvéɪʃ(ə)n] B1	8.
extinction 名 [ɪkstíŋ(k)ʃ(ə)n] B1	9.	decision-making 名 [dɪsíʒ(ə)nmèɪkɪŋ]	10.
according 形 [əkɔ́ːrdɪŋ] B1	従った	according to …	11.

be threatened with …	12.	care about …	13.
come to mind	14.	play a role in …	15.
each other	16.	ecosystem 名 [í:kousìstəm] B1	17.

A 【Comprehension 1】 Fill in the blanks in Japanese.

パラグラフごとの要点を整理しよう【思考力・判断力・表現力】

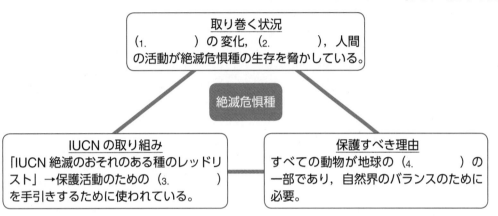

B 【Comprehension 2】 Answer the following questions in English.

本文のポイントについて答えよう【思考力・判断力・表現力】

1. What might endangered animals do in the near future?

----

2. What shows that more than 13,000 animal species are threatened with extinction?

C 【Key Sentences】 Fill in the blanks and translate the following sentences.

重要文について確認しよう【知識・技能】【思考力・判断力・表現力】

⑥ In addition to being animals, they are all endangered animals.

◆in addition to … は「動物であることに加えて，(1.　　　　 [日本語で]）でもある」ということ。

◆they＝(2.　　　 [英語で]），(3.　　　　 [英語2語で]），(4.　　　 [英語で]）。

訳：--

⑫ "Why **should** endangered species **be protected**?"

◆助動詞 should＋be＋過去分詞の形で，「～されるべきだ」という意味。

訳：--

Part 3 教科書 p.62 ◀意味のまとまりに注意して，本文全体を聞こう。 ◎1-36

4 ①There is an interesting survey. // ②One thousand people were asked / to donate some money / for endangered animals. // ③Almost all the people answered / that they would be interested in donating. // ④What kinds of animals / did they want to make a donation / to help? //

5 ⑤According to the survey, / 43 percent of the people / would donate / for the endangered animals / that they liked, / such as pandas and koalas. // ⑥On the other hand, / they would not donate / for animals / they didn't like, / such as snakes and lizards. // ⑦Most of them answered / that it was not fair / to help only attractive animals, though. //

6 ⑧It seems / that people like to protect animals / that they find attractive or cute. // ⑨Some companies tend to use such animals / in advertisements / to raise their sales. // ⑩It is true / that we are making efforts / to protect endangered animals. // ⑪However, / the animals that receive our protection / are often decided / by our personal preferences. //

◀意味のまとまりに注意して，本文全体を音読しよう。(151 Words)

Words and Phrases	新出単語・表現の意味を調べよう		
donate 動[dóuneɪt] B2	1.	donation 名 [dounéɪʃ(ə)n] B2	2.
make a donation	3.	lizard 名[lízərd]	4.
tend 動[ténd] B1	5.	tend to ～	6.
advertisement 名 [ædvərtáɪzmənt] A2	7.	protection 名 [prətékʃ(ə)n] B1	8.
preference 名 [préf(ə)r(ə)ns] B1	9.		

A 【Comprehension 1】 Fill in the blanks in Japanese.

パラグラフごとの要点を整理しよう【思考力・判断力・表現力】

調査を受けた1,000人中ほとんどが，寄付への（₁.　　　　）を示した。

半数近くが，自分が（₂.　　　　）な動物に寄付し，そうでない動物には寄付しようとしなかった。

人々は（₃.　　　　）で（₄.　　　　）と思う動物を保護したいと思う傾向がある。保護の対象となる動物は，人間の個人的な（₅.　　　　）に左右される。

B 【Comprehension 2】 Answer the following questions in English.

本文のポイントについて答えよう【思考力・判断力・表現力】

1. What did most people answer about donating for endangered animals?

   ----

2. Did many people answer that helping only attractive animals was fair?

   ----

3. How do we often decide the animals that receive our protection?

C 【Key Sentences】 Translate the following sentences.

重要文について確認しよう【知識・技能】【思考力・判断力・表現力】

⑤ According to the survey, 43 percent of the people would donate for the endangered animals (**that** they liked), such as pandas and koalas.

◆関係代名詞 that を含む節が先行詞 the endangered animals を修飾している。
◆ such as ... は，（好まれる）絶滅危惧動物の例を挙げている。

訳：--------

⑧ **It seems that** people like to protect animals (**that** they find attractive or cute).

◆ it seems that ... で「…であるようだ」という意味。
◆ find＋O＋C で「O が C だとわかる［思う］」という意味。find の目的語は animals で，先行詞となっている。

訳：--------

⑩ It is true that we are making efforts to protect endangered animals. **However,** the animals (that receive our protection) are often decided by our personal preferences.

◆ It は形式主語で that-節の内容が真主語。
◆ however は対比を示すディスコースマーカー。前の文に対して異なる観点から意見を対比させる。

訳：--------

Part 4 　教科書 p.63　◀意味のまとまりに注意して，本文全体を聞こう。　◎1-38

7 　①Why do we think / that bears and pandas are cute? // ②First, / they have human-like characteristics. // ③Second, / they live in a family setting, / like bears and their babies. // ④Lastly, / we like larger animals. // ⑤Most smaller species, / such as insects, / tend to be ignored. // ⑥Some people say / that conservation today / is for "beautiful and useful species only." // ⑦Is it good for us / to protect only those species? //

8 　⑧We should not forget / that human beings are / one of the species / on earth. // ⑨Human society is / part of the global ecosystem. // ⑩We gain a lot of benefits / from the natural environment / and from the ecosystem. // ⑪They are called / ecosystem services. // ⑫They are the foundation / of all food and agricultural systems. //

9 　⑬Our lives are closely connected / to ecosystem services. // ⑭By protecting the environment and endangered species, / we help / not only the endangered animals / but also ourselves. // ⑮We have to think about this: / "How can we live / in harmony with nature / on a healthy planet?" //

◀意味のまとまりに注意して，本文全体を音読しよう。(159 Words)

Words and Phrases　新出単語・表現の意味を調べよう			
human-like 形 [hjúːmənlàɪk]	1.	characteristic 名 [kæ̀rəktərístɪk] B1	2.
ignore 動 [ɪgnɔ́ːr] B1	3.	gain 動 [géɪn] B1	4.
benefit 名 [bénɪfɪt] B1	5.	agricultural 形 [æ̀grɪkʌ́ltʃ(ə)r(ə)l] B1	6.
not only A but also B	7.	harmony 名 [háːrməni] A2	8.
in harmony with …	9.		

A 【Comprehension 1】 Fill in the blanks in Japanese.

パラグラフごとの要点を整理しよう【思考力・判断力・表現力】

現代の自然保護に関する問題提起
美しくて（1.　　　　　　　）種だけを
保護することはよいのだろうか。

人間社会も地球の生態系の一部であり，
私たち人間は自然環境や生態系からの
恩恵＝(2.　　　　　　　　）を
受けている。

絶滅の危機にある動物だけでなく，私
たち自身も救うことになる。
「どのように自然と (3.　　　　　）して
健全な地球で生きていけるのか」とい
う問いを考えなければならない。

B 【Comprehension 2】 Answer the following questions in English.

本文のポイントについて答えよう【思考力・判断力・表現力】

1. Why do we tend to ignore smaller species for conservation?

   ----

2. What are benefits from the natural environment and the ecosystem called?

   ----

3. How do we help ourselves as well as the endangered animals?

C 【Key Sentences】 Fill in the blanks and translate the following sentences.

重要文について確認しよう【知識・技能】【思考力・判断力・表現力】

① Why do we think that bears and pandas are cute? First, **they** have human-like characteristics. Second, **they** live in a family setting, like bears and their babies. Lastly, we like larger animals.

◆ first（第一に），second（第二に），lastly（最後に）は列挙を示すディスコースマーカー。
　ここでは (1.　　　　　　　　[日本語で]）を列挙している。
◆ they＝(2.　　　　　　　[英語で]）and（3.　　　　　　[英語で]）。
訳：--

⑭ By protecting the environment and endangered species, we <u>help</u> **not only** <u>the endangered animals</u> **but also** <u>ourselves</u>.
V　　　　　　　　　　　　
O　　　　　　　　　O

◆ not only A but also B の A と B が，いずれも help の目的語となっている。
訳：--

Activity Plus 　教科書 p.68~p.69 　◀意味のまとまりに注意して，本文全体を聞こう。　◉1-40

①You are looking / at a poster / about saving polar bears. //

②Save the Polar Bear! //

③Do you know / that polar bears spend / most of their lives / on the sea ice / of the Arctic Ocean? // ④They hunt for food / and raise their babies / on the ice. //

⑤Due to climate change, / the sea ice is disappearing. // ⑥Because of this, / polar bears may become extinct / in the near future. // ⑦Their future is / in great danger. //

⑧Help Polar Bears, / an NGO, / wants to protect / polar bears. // ⑨It has started a five-year campaign / to raise awareness / about their situation. // ⑩We ask for your support. // ⑪Any donations will be welcomed. // ⑫The money will contribute / to the following five areas: //

⑬1. Tracking polar bear mothers // 　⑭2. Monitoring polar bear habitats //

⑮3. Mapping future polar bear habitats // 　⑯4. Understanding climate change //

⑰5. Preserving the Arctic food chain //

⑱You can help polar bears / and their polar home / by supporting Help Polar Bears. // ⑲We need your help. // ⑳If you are interested in this project, / please contact us / at https://www.helppolarbears.com. //

◀意味のまとまりに注意して，本文全体を音読しよう。(171 Words)

Words and Phrases　新出単語・表現の意味を調べよう			
Arctic 形 [ɑ́ːrktɪk] B2	1.	due to …	2.
because of …	3.	extinct 形 [ɪkstíŋ(k)t] B1	4.
be in danger	5.	campaign 名 [kæmpéɪn] B2	6.
raise awareness	7.	awareness 名 [əwéərnəs] B1	8.
contribute 動 [kəntríbjət] B1	9.	contribute to …	10.
monitor 動 [mɑ́(ː)nətər] B1	11.	preserve 動 [prɪzə́ːrv] B1	12.
chain 名 [tʃéɪn] A2	13.		

A 【Comprehension 1】 Fill in the blanks in Japanese.

要点を整理しよう【思考力・判断力・表現力】

アピール文	ホッキョクグマを救おう！
活動内容	［活動団体］Help Polar Bears （NGO 団体） ［主な活動］ホッキョクグマの保護 ［告知内容］５年間のキャンペーンの開始と援助のお願い ［寄付の用途］ １．母親クマの（1. 　　　　　） ２．生息地の（2. 　　　　　） ３．将来の生息地を示す（3. 　　　　）の作成 ４．（4. 　　　　）の変化の理解 ５．北極における（5. 　　　　　）の保存
問い合わせ先	https://www.helppolarbears.com

B 【Comprehension 2】 Answer the following questions in English.

本文のポイントについて答えよう【思考力・判断力・表現力】

1. Who made this poster?

   ----

2. Why has Help Polar Bears started a five-year campaign?

   ----

3. If you are interested in the project, what should you do?

C 【Key Sentences】 Fill in the blanks and translate the following sentences.

重要文について確認しよう【知識・技能】【思考力・判断力・表現力】

③ Do you know that polar bears spend **most of** their lives on the sea ice of the Arctic Ocean?

   ◆ most of ... は「…のほとんど」という意味。

   訳：---

⑥ Because of this, polar bears may become extinct in the near future.

   ◆ Because of this ＝（1. 　　　　　[日本語で]）のため（2. 　　　　　[日本語で]）こと。

   訳：---

⑨ It has started a five-year campaign to raise awareness about their situation.

   ◆ It ＝（3. 　　　　　[英語3語で]），their ＝（4. 　　　　　[英語2語で]）。

   訳：---

Part 1 教科書 p.74〜p.77 ◁意味のまとまりに注意して，本文全体を聞こう。 ◉1-42

① You want to go / to a *Curious George* exhibit / with your family. // ② You are looking at the exhibit website. //

③ Museum of Culture and Science //

④ Special Exhibit Events // ⑤ Let's Have Fun with *Curious George*! //

⑥ Do you know / a cute little monkey / that always gets himself into trouble? //

⑦ Yes, / it's George, / Curious George! // ⑧ He is a good little monkey / and always very curious. //

⑨ This curiosity leads him / to meet a man / with a yellow hat / and to travel / from Africa / to get a new home / in a zoo. // ⑩ His curiosity gets George into trouble, / but it always helps him / out of it. //

⑪ Let's experience the world / of *Curious George*! // ⑫ In these exhibit events, / you can see buildings and places / from the *Curious George* books / and animations. // ⑬ Experience a lot of new things / with curiosity. // ⑭ These special events / will give you a wonderful experience / you won't forget! //

⑮ Special appearance by George, / along with one of his stories, / at 10 a.m. and 1 p.m.! //

⑯ TICKETS // ⑰ · $21 for adults from 13 to 64 // ⑱ · $19 for adults 65 and over //

⑲ · $16 for children from 2 to 12 / (Children under 2 are free.) //

⑳ A ticket includes / one special 45-minute documentary movie. //

㉑ TIME // ㉒ · Monday through Saturday / from 10 a.m. to 5 p.m. //

㉓ · Sunday / from noon to 6 p.m. //

㉔ PLACE // ㉕ Museum of Culture and Science //

㉖ 401 North Second Street, Green Forest, FL 333XX //

◁意味のまとまりに注意して，本文全体を音読しよう。(232 Words)

Words and Phrases 新出単語・表現の意味を調べよう			
Curious George [kjúəriəs dʒɔ́ːrdʒ]	キュリアス・ジョージ	exhibit 图[ɪgzíbət]	1.

get ... into trouble	2.	curiosity 名 [kjùəriá(:)səti] B1	3.
help A out of B	4.	include 動 [ɪnklúːd] A2	5.
documentary 形 [dà(:)kjəmént(ə)ri]	6.		

A 【**Comprehension 1**】 Fill in the blanks in Japanese.

要点を整理しよう【思考力・判断力・表現力】

特別イベントの案内

・チケット代

2歳〜12歳	13歳〜64歳	65歳以上
16ドル	(1.　　　　) ドル	19ドル

*45分の (2.　　　　)，1回分が無料

・開館時間

月〜土曜日	日曜日
10時〜5時	12時〜(3.　　　) 時

『おさるのジョージ』の世界を体験できる

かわいい小猿で，いつも（4.　　　　）いっぱい。黄色い帽子のおじさんに出会い，アフリカから（5.　　　　）にある新しい家へ旅をする。

B 【**Comprehension 2**】 Answer the following questions in English.

本文のポイントについて答えよう【思考力・判断力・表現力】

1. What happens at 10 a.m. and 1 p.m. during the events?

....

2. If two high school students and one elementary school student visit the event, how much does it cost?

....

C 【**Key Sentences**】 Fill in the blanks and translate the following sentences.

重要文について確認しよう【知識・技能】【思考力・判断力・表現力】

⑥ Do you know a cute little monkey (**that** always gets himself into trouble)?

◆ that は関係代名詞で，先行詞は a cute little monkey。

訳：...

⑩ It always helps him out of it.

◆文頭の It＝(1.　　　　　[英語で])，文末の it＝(2.　　　　　　[英語で])。

◆ him は (Curious) George を指す。

訳：...

Part 2 教科書 p.78 意味のまとまりに注意して，本文全体を聞こう。 1-44

①While millions of people know *Curious George*, / not many people know / about the careers / of his creators. // ②How did they create / one of the world's most famous monkeys? //

① ③Hans Augusto Rey was born / in Germany / in 1898 / to Jewish parents. // ④He grew up / a few blocks / from a zoo. // ⑤So he developed a lifelong love / for animals and drawing. // ⑥He met a young Jewish girl, / Margret, / at her sister's birthday party. // ⑦Later, / Margret left her hometown / to study art, / and they lost touch / for a while. //

② ⑧In 1935, / Hans and Margret met again / in Brazil. // ⑨Hans was doing some family business. // ⑩Margret was escaping the political climate / in Germany. // ⑪They decided to start working together. // ⑫They soon fell in love / and got married / in August. //

③ ⑬In 1936, / Hans and Margret traveled / to Paris, France. // ⑭They enjoyed Paris so much / that they decided to stay there. // ⑮Then Hans had a chance / to publish some of his animal drawings / in a French magazine. // ⑯His drawings became quite popular. // ⑰That made the publisher decide to publish / Hans' first children's book, / *Raffy and the Nine Monkeys*, / in 1939. //

意味のまとまりに注意して，本文全体を音読しよう。(184 Words)

Words and Phrases	新出単語・表現の意味を調べよう		
millions of ...	1.	creator 图 [kriéɪtər] B1	2.
Hans Augusto Rey [hǽns ɔːgʌ́stə réɪ]	ハンス・アウグスト・レイ	Jewish 形 [dʒúːɪʃ]	3.
lifelong 形 [láɪflɔ̀ːŋ] B1	4.	Margret [máːrgrət]	マーガレット
lose touch	5.	for a while	6.
fall in love	7.	marry 動 [mǽri] A2	8.
publish 動 [pʌ́blɪʃ] A2	9.	publisher 图 [pʌ́blɪʃər] B1	10.
Raffy [rǽfi]	ラフィー		

A 【Comprehension 1】 Fill in the blanks in Japanese.

パラグラフごとの要点を整理しよう【思考力・判断力・表現力】

1898年	ハンス・アウグスト・レイがドイツで生まれる。
▼	マーガレットと, 彼女の姉の（1.　　　　　）で出会う。
1935年	2人は（2.　　　　　）で再会。8月に結婚。
▼	
1936年	2人は（3.　　　　）に移住。
▼	ハンスの描く動物の絵が人気になる。
1939年	ハンスの最初の児童書が（4.　　　　）される。

B 【Comprehension 2】 Answer the following questions in English.

本文のポイントについて答えよう【思考力・判断力・表現力】

1. Where was Hans Augusto Rey born?

----

2. Why did Margret leave her hometown?

----

3. What was the name of Hans' first children's book?

C 【Key Sentences】 Fill in the blanks and translate the following sentences.

重要文について確認しよう【知識・技能】【思考力・判断力・表現力】

⑦ Later, Margret left her hometown / to study art, and they lost touch for a while.
   ◆ Later は（1.　　　　　　　　　[日本語で]）の後ということ。
   ◆ to study art は目的を表す to-不定詞の副詞用法。
   ◆ they＝Hans and Margret。
   訳: ---

⑭ They enjoyed Paris **so** much **that** they decided to stay there.
   ◆ so … that ～は「とても…なので～」の意味。
   ◆ They, they＝Hans and Margret, there＝（2.　　　　[英語で]）。
   訳: ---

⑰ That <u>made</u> <u>the publisher</u> <u>decide</u> to publish Hans' first children's book, *Raffy and the Nine Monkeys*, in 1939.
   （V　O　C）
   ◆ That は（3.　　　　　　　　[日本語で]）ということ。
   ◆ make＋O＋C（＝原形不定詞）は「O に C させる」の意味。
   ◆ children's book, *Raffy and the Nine Monkeys* のコンマは同格を表す。
   訳: ---

Part 3 教科書 p.79 ◁意味のまとまりに注意して，本文全体を聞こう。 ◎1-46

4 ①Only a few months / after Hans' book was published, / World War II broke out / in 1939. // ②Since they were German Jews / in Paris, / Hans and Margret Rey felt / they would be in danger. // ③In June 1940, / the Nazi army / was rapidly approaching Paris. //

5 ④There were no more trains, / and the Reys didn't own a car. // ⑤They had to find a way / to get away / from Paris. // ⑥Hans hurried over / to a bicycle shop, / but there were no bicycles / for them. // ⑦Only spare parts were available. // ⑧That night, / Hans put the parts together / to make two bicycles. //

6 ⑨Early in the morning / of June 12, / 1940, / the Reys set off / on their bicycles. // ⑩They took very little with them: / warm clothes, / some food / and some unpublished manuscripts / of children's books. // ⑪They included one special book, / *Fifi: The Adventures of a Monkey*. // ⑫It was just 48 hours / before the Nazi army marched / into Paris. // ⑬They were finally / among the millions of refugees / trying to run away / to the south. //

◁意味のまとまりに注意して，本文全体を音読しよう。(166 Words)

Words and Phrases	新出単語・表現の意味を調べよう		
only a few …	1.	break out	2.
Jew 名[dʒúː]	3.	Nazi 形[náːtsi]	4.
army 名[áːrmi] B1	5.	approach 動[əpróutʃ] B2	6.
get away from …	7.	spare 形[spéər] B2	8.
available 形[əvéɪləb(ə)l] B1	9.	put … together	10.
set off	11.	unpublished 形[ʌnpʌ́blɪʃt]	12.
manuscript 名[mǽnjəskrìpt]	13.	Fifi [fíːfi]	フィフィ
march 動[máːrtʃ] B1	14.	refugee 名[rèfjudʒíː] B2	15.
run away	16.		

A 【Comprehension 1】 Fill in the blanks in Japanese.

パラグラフごとの要点を整理しよう【思考力・判断力・表現力】

1939年	ハンスの最初の児童書が出版される。
▼	数か月後，（1. 　　　　　　　　　）が起こる。
1940年6月	ナチスの軍隊が急速にパリに近づいてくる。
⋮	電車も車もなかったので，（2. 　　　）でパリから逃げることを決める。
【12日朝】	温かい服と食べ物と（3. 　　　　　　　）だけを持って出発する。
⋮	何百万人もの（4. 　　　）とともに，南へ逃げる。
【48時間後】	ナチスがパリへ侵攻する。

B 【Comprehension 2】 Answer the following questions in English.

本文のポイントについて答えよう【思考力・判断力・表現力】

1. What happened only a few months after Hans' first children's book was published?

---

2. What did Hans do after he went to a bicycle shop?

---

3. When did the Nazi army march into Paris?

C 【Key Sentences】 Translate the following sentences.

重要文について確認しよう【知識・技能】【思考力・判断力・表現力】

② **Since** they were German Jews in Paris, Hans and Margret Rey <u>felt</u> <u>they would</u>
V　　　　O
be in danger.
   ◆接続詞 Since は理由を表す節を導いている。they＝Hans and Margret Rey。
   ◆ felt の目的語は (that) they would be in danger。
   訳:

⑤ They had to find a way to get away from Paris.
   ◆音の変化に注意。had to（音が消える），find a / get away（音がつながる）。
   訳:

⑬ They were finally among the millions of refugees (trying to run away to the
   S　V　　　C
   south).
   ◆ among ... が be-動詞に対する補語になっている S＋V＋C の文。
   ◆ trying ... は分詞の形容詞用法で，the millions of refugees を修飾する。
   訳:

Part 4 教科書 p.80 🔊意味のまとまりに注意して，本文全体を聞こう。 ⊙1-48

7 ①Hans and Margret slept / in barns / and on floors / of restaurants / on the way south. // ②Finally, / they came across running trains. // ③This was their chance / to get out of France. // ④However, / a checkpoint officer became suspicious / of their German accents. // ⑤When he searched their bags / and found the manuscript of *Fifi*, / he was sure / that they were not German spies. // ⑥Thanks to their cute little monkey, / the Reys passed through Spain / and made it out of Europe / to Brazil / by ship. // ⑦After reaching Brazil, / they continued on / to New York. //

8 ⑧In October 1940, / Hans and Margret arrived safely / in America. // ⑨One year later, / *Fifi: The Adventures of a Monkey* / was published / in America / under the new name: / *Curious George*. //

9 ⑩Think of all the smiles / around the world / that have been made / by one mischievous little monkey! // ⑪*Curious George* / seems to reflect / what his creators experienced / while they were escaping the Nazis. // ⑫Who knew / such a historic adventure / was behind a warm character / of innocent mischief? //

🔊意味のまとまりに注意して，本文全体を音読しよう。(165 Words)

Words and Phrases	新出単語・表現の意味を調べよう		
barn 名[bá:rn] B2	1.	on the way …	2.
come across …	3.	checkpoint 名 [tʃékpɔ̀ɪnt] B2	4.
suspicious 形 [səspíʃəs] B2	5.	accent 名 [ǽksent] B1	6.
search 動 [sə́:rtʃ] B1	7.	make it	8.
mischievous 形 [místʃɪvəs]	9.	reflect 動 [riflékt] A2	10.
historic 形 [hɪstɔ́:rɪk] B1	11.	innocent 形 [ínəs(ə)nt] B1	12.
mischief 名 [místʃɪf] B1	13.		

A 【Comprehension 1】 Fill in the blanks in Japanese.

パラグラフごとの要点を整理しよう【思考力・判断力・表現力】

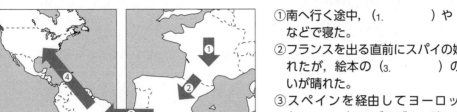

① 南へ行く途中，（1.　　　　）や（2.　　　　）などで寝た。
② フランスを出る直前にスパイの嫌疑をかけられたが，絵本の（3.　　　　）のおかげで疑いが晴れた。
③ スペインを経由してヨーロッパを脱出。（4.　　　　）でブラジルへ渡った。
④ 無事にアメリカに到着。その後『おさるのジョージ』を出版した。

B 【Comprehension 2】 Answer the following questions in English.

本文のポイントについて答えよう【思考力・判断力・表現力】

1. Where did Hans and Margret sleep on the way south?

---

2. In what year was the book *Curious George* first published?

---

3. Has *Curious George* been loved by people around the world?

C 【Key Sentences】 Fill in the blanks and translate the following sentences.

重要文について確認しよう【知識・技能】【思考力・判断力・表現力】

③ This was their chance (to get out of France).

◆ This は（1.　　　　　　　　　　　　　[日本語で]）ということ。
◆ to get out of France は their chance を修飾する to-不定詞の形容詞用法。
訳：---

⑩ Think of all the smiles around the world (**that** have been made by one mischievous little monkey)!

◆ that は関係代名詞で，先行詞は all the smiles (around the world)。
◆ have been made は受け身の現在完了形。『おさるのジョージ』誕生から現在までの継続を表す。
訳：---

⑪ *Curious George* seems to reflect **what** his creators experienced while they were escaping the Nazis.

◆関係代名詞 what を用いた what his creators experienced は（2.　　　　　　　[日本語で]）の意味。reflect の目的語となっている。
◆この文は It（3.　　　[英語で]）that *Curious George* reflects what his creators experienced while they were escaping the Nazis. と書きかえることができる。
訳：---

Activity Plus 教科書 p.84～p.85 ◁意味のまとまりに注意して，本文全体を聞こう。 ◎1-50

①In 2017, / the *Curious George* documentary / *MONKEY BUSINESS* / was released / by a film director, / Ema Ryan Yamazaki. // ②You are listening to an interview / with her. //

③Q1) What made you decide / to become a film director? //

④When I was in high school, / I began telling stories / with a camera. // ⑤I realized / I had a passion / for sharing / what I found interesting / with others. // ⑥So I decided / to study filmmaking / in college, / and it has led me / to this career. //

⑦Q2) Why did you choose / *Curious George* / and its creators / as the theme / of your work? //

⑧I happened to learn / about the creators / of *Curious George* / from a friend. // ⑨I loved *Curious George*, / but I didn't know anything / about his creators / before then. // ⑩I was inspired / when I knew / that they experienced hardships / but left behind wonderful stories / and a cute character. // ⑪I thought / that their story should be shared / with the world. //

⑫Q3) Please give your message / to high school students. //

⑬I was lucky / to find my passion / in high school, / and now / I have a career / in doing what I enjoy the most. // ⑭I learned a lot / from the creators / of *Curious George*. // ⑮I hope / your curiosity will drive you / to discover / what you like / and to see life / as an adventure! //

◁意味のまとまりに注意して，本文全体を音読しよう。(180 Words)

Words and Phrases 新出単語・表現の意味を調べよう			
director 名[dəréktər] A2	1.	Ema Ryan [émə ráɪən]	エマ・ライアン
passion 名[pǽʃ(ə)n] B1	2.	share A with B	3.
filmmaking 名[fílmmèɪkɪŋ]	4.	lead A to B	5.
happen to ～	6.	inspire 動[ɪnspáɪər] B1	7.
leave … behind	8.	see A as B	9.

A 【Comprehension 1】 Fill in the blanks in Japanese.

要点を整理しよう【思考力・判断力・表現力】

Q1) なぜ映画監督になることを決意したか。	高校生のとき，カメラを使ったストーリーテリングを始めたのがきっかけで，興味を持ったことを人に伝えるという（1.　　　　）があることに気付いたことが今の仕事につながっている。
Q2) なぜ作品のテーマに『おさるのジョージ』とその作者を選んだか。	作者は（2.　　　　）を経験したが，すばらしいストーリーとかわいいキャラクターを残した。このことを世界と（3.　　　　）すべきだと思ったから。
Q3) 高校生へのメッセージは？	好奇心を持つことで何か好きなことを発見し，人生を（4.　　　　）と考えるようになる。

B 【Comprehension 2】 Answer the following questions in English.

本文のポイントについて答えよう【思考力・判断力・表現力】

1. What did Ema realize when she was in high school?

   ----

2. Did Ema know about the creators of *Curious George*?

   ----

3. What does Ema hope for high school students?

C 【Key Sentences】 Fill in the blank and translate the following sentences.

重要文について確認しよう【知識・技能】【思考力・判断力・表現力】

⑤ I realized I had a passion for **sharing** what I found interesting **with** others.

◆ realized の目的語は (that) I had a passion for …。sharing A with B の A に関係代名詞 what を用いた what I found interesting が入る。found＋O＋C の O（先行詞）が関係代名詞 what に含まれている。

訳：--

⑩ I was inspired / when I knew that they experienced hardships **but** left behind wonderful stories **and** a cute character.

◆ when-節中の knew の目的語は that-節。but は動詞 experienced … と left …をつなぐ等位接続詞で「経験したが，残した」という意味。and は wonderful stories と a cute character をつなぐ等位接続詞。

訳：--

⑮ I hope your curiosity will drive you to discover what you like and to see life as an adventure.

◆ hope の目的語は (that) your curiosity will ～。drive you to ～ の to-不定詞の名詞用法 2 つが and で並列されている。一つは to discover … で，もう一つが to（1.　　　　[英語で]）。discover の目的語に関係代名詞 what を含む what you like が入っている。

訳：--

Part 1 教科書 p.90～p.91 ◁意味のまとまりに注意して，本文全体を聞こう。 ◉2-2

① You are listening to a poster presentation / about "The Poorest President in the World." //

② The Poorest President in the World // ③ Jose Mujica //

④ Born: May 20, 1935 // ⑤ Family: wife, pets and other animals //

⑥ His Life —— Very Unusual for a President! //

⑦ Mr. Mujica … //

⑧ · leads a very simple life / near Montevideo, / the capital of Uruguay. //

⑨ · loves taking care of animals and plants / on his farm. //

⑩ · likes reading very much / and gives most of his books / to schools later. //

⑪ · never wears expensive clothes / and never wears a tie, / even with his suit. //

⑫ · lived on a low salary / even when he was the president. //

⑬ · didn't live in the president's official residence, / and didn't use the president's official car / or the president's official plane. //

⑭ Mr. Mujica was born / into a poor family / in Uruguay / in 1935. // ⑮ His father died / when he was seven, / and his mother supported the family. // ⑯ When he was a university student, / the economy of his country / was in a bad condition / and the difference of quality of life / between the rich and the poor / was large. // ⑰ He decided to do something / to help his country. // ⑱ After he graduated from university, / he protested against the government. // ⑲ He was arrested several times, / but he never lost hope. // ⑳ He was finally released / in 1985 / and became a politician / ten years later. // ㉑ In 2009, / he was elected president / of Uruguay. // ◁意味のまとまりに注意して，本文全体を音読しよう。(232 Words)

Words and Phrases	新出単語・表現の意味を調べよう		
Jose Mujica [houséɪ məhíkə]	ホセ・ムヒカ	lead a life	1.
Montevideo [mà(:)ntəvədéɪou]	モンテビデオ	Uruguay [jʊ́arəgwàɪ]	2.
take care of …	3.	live on …	4.

salary 名 [sǽl(ə)ri] B2	5.	official 形 [əfíʃ(ə)l] A2	6.
residence 名 [rézɪd(ə)ns] B2	7.	economy 名 [ɪkɑ́(ː)nəmi] B1	8.
protest 動 [prətést] B2	9.	arrest 動 [ərést] B1	10.
elect 動 [ɪlékt] B2	11.		

A 【Comprehension 1】 Fill in the blanks in Japanese.

要点を整理しよう【思考力・判断力・表現力】

(1.　　　) 年	ホセ・ムヒカはウルグアイの貧しい家庭に生まれる。
(2.　　　) 歳のとき	父親が亡くなる。
大学生のとき	国の状況を見て，ある決心をする。
大学卒業後	政府への抗議活動で逮捕される。
(3.　　　) 年	解放される。
(4.　　　) 年	政治家になる。
(5.　　　) 年	ウルグアイ大統領に選出される。

B 【Comprehension 2】 Answer the following questions in English.

本文のポイントについて答えよう【思考力・判断力・表現力】

1. What did Mujica decide to do when he was a university student?

---

2. Why was Mujica arrested several times?

C 【Key Sentences】 Fill in the blanks and translate the following sentences.

重要文について確認しよう【知識・技能】【思考力・判断力・表現力】

⑯ The difference of quality of life between the rich and the poor <u>was</u> large.
　　◆下線部の主語を名詞1語で抜き出すと（1.　　　　　[英語で]）。
　　◆the＋形容詞は「…な人々」の意味。the rich は（2.　　　　　[日本語で]）という意味になる。
　　訳：---

㉑ He was elected president of Uruguay.
　　◆elect の補語となる役職名（president of Uruguay）にはふつう冠詞を付けない。
　　訳：---

Part 2 教科書 p.92 ◀意味のまとまりに注意して，本文全体を聞こう。 ◎2-4

①Why did Jose Mujica come to be called / "the poorest president in the world"? //

②What does he think / about that? //

① ③Laundry hangs / outside the house. // ④Water comes / from a well / in a yard / full of tall grass. // ⑤Only two police officers / and a dog / keep watch outside. // ⑥This is the house / of a former president / of Uruguay, / Jose Mujica. // ⑦It is on a farm / outside the capital, / Montevideo. //

② ⑧Mujica went to work / from this residence / even during his service / as president. // ⑨He didn't want to move / to the official residence / when he was elected / in 2009. // ⑩He donated / most of his salary / to charities. // ⑪His monthly income was / about 1,000 dollars. // ⑫It was very low / for a leader / of a country, / so he was seen / as "the poorest president in the world." //

③ ⑬"I'm called the poorest president, / but I don't feel poor," / Mujica says. // ⑭"A president is a high-level official / who is elected / to carry out his or her duty. // ⑮A president is not a king, / not a god. // ⑯A president is a civil servant. // ⑰The ideal way of living / is to live / like the majority of people." //

◀意味のまとまりに注意して，本文全体を音読しよう。 (188 Words)

Words and Phrases	新出単語・表現の意味を調べよう		
laundry 名 [lɔ́:ndri] B2	1.	hang 動 [hǽŋ] B1	2.
come from …	3.	keep watch	4.
monthly 形 [mʌ́nθli] B1	5.	income 名 [ínkʌ̀m] B1	6.
high-level 形 [hàɪlév(ə)l]	7.	carry out …	8.
duty 名 [djú:ti] B1	9.	civil 形 [sív(ə)l] B1	10.
servant 名 [sə́:rv(ə)nt] B2	11.	majority 名 [mədʒɔ́:rəti] B1	12.

A 【Comprehension 1】 Fill in the blanks in Japanese.

パラグラフごとの要点を整理しよう【思考力・判断力・表現力】

ムヒカの家	ムヒカの大統領時代
・外には（1.　　　　）が干され，水は庭の（2.　　　　）から引いている。 ・ムヒカの家は首都から外れた（3.　　　　）にある。	・給料の大部分を（4.　　　　　　　）に寄付していたため，月収は少なかった。 ・人はムヒカを「世界でいちばん（5.　　　）大統領」と呼んだが，彼自身はそう感じていなかった。

B 【Comprehension 2】 Answer the following questions in English.

本文のポイントについて答えよう【思考力・判断力・表現力】

1. How many police officers keep watch outside Mujica's house?

2. What did Mujica donate most of his salary to?

3. How much was Mujica's monthly income when he was a president?

C 【Key Sentences】 Fill in the blank and translate the following sentences.

重要文について確認しよう【知識・技能】【思考力・判断力・表現力】

⑭ A president is a high-level official (**who** is elected to carry out his or her duty).

◆関係代名詞 who の先行詞は a high-level official。

訳：

⑮ A president is not a king, not a god. A president is a civil servant.

◆先の文で否定文（is not a king, not a god）を使い，次の文で肯定文（is a civil servant）を使うことで，相対するものを並べる対照法が用いられている。短いフレーズを用いることで，わかりやすく意図を強調する。

訳：

    S   V   C

⑰ The ideal way of living is to live like the majority of people.

◆ideal way of living は（1.　　　　　　　　　[日本語で]）の意味。

◆like ... 「…のように，…と同様に」。この like は前置詞として扱われる。

訳：

Part 3 教科書 p.93 🔊意味のまとまりに注意して，本文全体を聞こう。 ◉2-6

④ ①In April 2016, / Mujica was invited / to Japan / for the first time / because a Japanese publisher had just begun / to sell the book, / *The Poorest President in the World*. // ②He gave a speech / to young Japanese people / at Tokyo University of Foreign Studies. // ③In his casual clothes, / he didn't look like someone / who had been a president / of a country / for five years. //

⑤ ④Mujica delivered a message / about happiness and poverty. // ⑤In his address, / he stressed the importance / of love / for our happiness. // ⑥He said / that it is the most important thing / in the world / for us people. // ⑦"If people cannot share / the feeling of love / with their family, / friends / or neighbors, / they are poor. // ⑧The greatest poverty / in this world / is loneliness." //

⑥ ⑨According to Mujica, / poverty is not about what we have / or how much we have, / not a matter of wealth. // ⑩"I'm not the poorest president. // ⑪I can live well / with what I have. // ⑫The poorest person is the one / who needs a lot to live." //

🔊意味のまとまりに注意して，本文全体を音読しよう。 (168 Words)

Words and Phrases 新出単語・表現の意味を調べよう			
for the first time	1.	give a speech	2.
casual 形 [kǽʒuəl] B1	3.	deliver 動 [dɪlívər] B1	4.
poverty 名 [pá(:)vərti] B1	5.	stress 動 [strés] B2	6.
loneliness 名 [lóʊnlinəs] B2	7.	wealth 名 [wélθ] A2	8.

A 【**Comprehension 1**】 Fill in the blanks in Japanese.

パラグラフごとの要点を整理しよう【思考力・判断力・表現力】

ムヒカ来日時，大学での講演
ムヒカのメッセージ：(1.　　　　　) と貧困について
・幸福には（2.　　　　） が大切。 ・この世界で最大の貧困は（3.　　　　） である。 ・貧困とは，何を持っているか，（4.　　　　　） 持っているかではなく，（5.　　　　） の問題 　ではない。最も貧しい人というのは，生きるために多くを必要とする人である。

B 【**Comprehension 2**】 Answer the following questions in English.

本文のポイントについて答えよう【思考力・判断力・表現力】

1. Why was Mujica invited to Japan for the first time?

　---

2. According to Mujica, what is the greatest poverty in this world?

　---

3. According to Mujica, why does not he think of himself as the poorest president?

C 【**Key Sentences**】 Translate the following sentences.

重要文について確認しよう【知識・技能】【思考力・判断力・表現力】

① In April 2016, Mujica was invited to Japan for the first time because a Japanese publisher **had** just **begun** to sell the book, *The Poorest President in the World*.

　◆had just begun は過去完了形。「(過去のその時点までに) ちょうど〜し始めた」という過去のある時点までの動作の完了を表している。

　訳: ---

③ In his casual clothes, he didn't look like <u>someone</u> (**who** had been a president of a country for five years).

　◆関係代名詞の節内で had been a president と過去完了形になっている。主節の動詞 didn't look like ...「…のように見えなかった」という過去の時点より以前に，「5 年間，大統領であった」という状態を表している。

　訳: ---

⑦ If people cannot share the feeling of love with their **family**, **friends** or **neighbors**, they are poor.

　◆family, friends or neighbors と 3 つの語を並べることで文にリズム感を生み出し，聞き手の印象に残す効果がある。このように 3 つの語句の並置は英語のスピーチではよく用いられる。

　◆share A with B「A を B と分かち合う，共有する」。

　訳: ---

Part 4 教科書 p.94 ◁意味のまとまりに注意して，本文全体を聞こう。◎2-8

7 ①Mujica thinks highly of educating young people. // ②As a politician, / he believes / that good education has the power / to change the world / in the future. // ③Every time / he visits a foreign country, / he gives a speech / to young people, / especially university students. //

8 ④In Tokyo, / Mujica said / that Japanese students should ask themselves / what happiness is / and what poverty is. // ⑤He told them / that wealth is not what matters most, / and that we should not spend / all of our time / worrying about material things. // ⑥He stressed / that life is not only about earning money. // ⑦His words greatly impressed / the young people / of Japan. //

9 ⑧Japan is a highly developed country, / and we are surrounded / by various kinds of consumer goods / and high-tech products. // ⑨Japan has pursued economic growth / for decades, / but many people say / they are not satisfied. // ⑩A survey shows / that people's sense of happiness / in Japan / is not very high / among the industrialized nations. // ⑪Jose Mujica's message / teaches us / very important things / about how we should think / about happiness. //

◁意味のまとまりに注意して，本文全体を音読しよう。(169 Words)

Words and Phrases 新出単語・表現の意味を調べよう			
think highly of ...	1.	educate 動 [édʒəkèɪt] B1	2.
every time ...	3.	spend ... 〜ing	4.
worry about ...	5.	material 形 [mətíəriəl]	6.
consumer 名 [kənsjú:məɾ] B1	7.	high-tech 形 [hàɪték] B2	8.
pursue 動 [pəɾsjú:] A2	9.	economic 形 [ìːkəná(:)mɪk] B1	10.
growth 名 [gróʊθ] B1	11.	for decades	12.
satisfied 形 [sætɪsfàɪd] B1	13.	industrialize 動 [ɪndʌ́striəlàɪz] B2	14.

A 【Comprehension 1】 Fill in the blanks in Japanese.

パラグラフごとの要点を整理しよう【思考力・判断力・表現力】

(1.　　　　　) としてムヒカが信じていること よい (2.　　　　　) は未来の世界を変える力がある。		日本の今の状況
<u>ムヒカが若い人に伝えたいこと</u> (3.　　　　　) なものに気を取られて，私たちのすべての時間を費やすべきではない。人生はお金を (4.　　　　　) ことだけではない。	⇔	(5.　　　　　) 国になり，私たちはたくさんの消費財や (6.　　　　) 製品に囲まれている。日本は経済成長をずっと追い求めてきたが，多くの人は自分たちは (7.　　　　　　　　) と言う。

B 【Comprehension 2】 Answer the following questions in English.

本文のポイントについて答えよう【思考力・判断力・表現力】

1. What does Mujica think highly of?

---

2. According to Mujica, what should Japanese students do?

---

3. Has Japan pursued economic growth for long?

C 【Key Sentences】 Translate the following sentences.

重要文について確認しよう【知識・技能】【思考力・判断力・表現力】

④ In Tokyo, Mujica said / that Japanese students should <u>ask</u> <u>themselves</u> <u>what happiness is</u> and <u>what poverty is</u>.

(V) (O) (O)

(O)

◆疑問詞で始まる what happiness is と what poverty is の節が，動詞 ask の直接目的語となっている。

訳：---

⑤ He <u>told</u> <u>them</u> <u>that wealth is not what matters most</u>, and <u>that we should not spend all of our time worrying about material things</u>.

(V) (O₁) (O₂) (O₂)

◆下線部 2 か所の that-節は told の目的語になる。and で並列する場合，後ろの that-節は and that となり，この that は省略できないことに注意する。

◆ what matters most の matters は動詞。この what は先行詞を含む関係代名詞で「…であること[もの]」と訳す。

訳：---

⑪ Jose Mujica's message teaches <u>us</u> <u>very important things</u> (about how we should think about happiness).

(O₁) (O₂)

◆ teach＋O₁＋O₂は「(人) に (物) を教える」の意味。

◆ about how we should think ...「私たちがどのように考えるべきかについて」。疑問詞 how で始まる節が前置詞 about の目的語になっている。

訳：---

Activity Plus 教科書 p.98〜p.99 ◁意味のまとまりに注意して，本文全体を聞こう。 ◉2-10

①After a university student listened to Mujica's speech, / he studied happiness / in various countries. // ②He made a report / to present in class. //

③The United Nations / has published the World Happiness Report / every year / since 2012. // ④It is a survey / of the state / of global happiness, / and it ranks more than 150 countries / by their happiness levels. //

⑤The state of happiness / in this report / comes from several kinds of data: / GDP per person, / healthy life expectancy, / and data / from 1,000 people / in each country / about happiness. // ⑥The questions ask people / to rate several parts / of their lives / by using numbers / from zero to ten. // ⑦Zero is the worst possible life / and ten is the best. // ⑧The following are the results / from some of the past few years. //

⑨Three or four of the top five / each year / are Northern European countries. // ⑩They are thought / to be the most highly developed welfare countries / in the world. // ⑪Most people in these countries feel / that they are healthy, / comfortable / and happy. //

⑫On the other hand, / Japan ranks much lower / regarding happiness. // ⑬It is the lowest / among the G7 nations. // ⑭Japan is one of the leading countries / in some ways, / for example, / in economy and technology. // ⑮However, / Japanese people do not rank very high / for feeling healthy, / comfortable / and happy. // ⑯What is important / for us / to feel happy? //

◁意味のまとまりに注意して，本文全体を音読しよう。(222 Words)

Words and Phrases 新出単語・表現の意味を調べよう			
United Nations [juːnàɪtɪd néɪʃ(ə)nz]	1.	rank A by B	2.
data 名 [déɪtə] B2	3.	per 前 [pəːr] B1	4.
expectancy 名 [ɪkspékt(ə)nsi]	5.	rate 動 [réɪt] A2	6.
Denmark [dénmɑːrk]	7.	Norway [nɔ́ːrwèɪ]	8.

Switzerland [swítsərlənd]	9.	Netherlands [néðərlən(d)z]	10.
Iceland [áıslənd]	11.	welfare 名 [wélfèər] B2	12.
regarding 前 [rıgáːrdıŋ] B1	13.		

A 【Comprehension 1】 Fill in the blanks in Japanese.

要点を整理しよう【思考力・判断力・表現力】

世界幸福度報告
・2012年以来，（1.　　　）によって実施されている。
・（2.　　　）か国以上の国が順位付けされる。
・一人当たりの（3.　　　）や（4.　　　），国民の幸福に関するデータなどが使用される。
・各国1,000人が自身の生活について，点数を付ける。

トップ5には（5.　　　）の国々がランクイン。
これらの国の人々は，自分たちは（6.　　　）で快適で幸せだと感じている。

一方で，日本はずっと順位が低く，（7.　　　）の国々の中でも最も低い。

B 【Comprehension 2】 Answer the following questions in English.

本文のポイントについて答えよう【思考力・判断力・表現力】

1. What has the United Nations published every year since 2012?

   ....

2. What are the high-ranking Northern European countries thought to be?

   ....

C 【Key Sentences】 Fill in the blanks and translate the following sentences.

重要文について確認しよう【知識・技能】【思考力・判断力・表現力】

⑥ The questions **ask** people **to** rate several parts of their lives by using numbers from zero to ten.

  ◆ ask＋O＋to ～ 「人に～するように求める」。
  ◆ by using numbers 「数を使うことによって」。by は前置詞なので，後に続くのは名詞または動名詞。
  訳 : ....

⑦ Zero is the worst possible life and ten is the best.

  ◆ best の後には possible （1.　　　[英語で]）が省略されている。
  ◆ worst は形容詞（2.　　　[英語で]）の最上級。比較級は（3.　　　[英語で]）。
  訳 : ....

Part 1 教科書 p.104〜p.105 🔊意味のまとまりに注意して，本文全体を聞こう。 ◎2-12

①You want to learn / something about Seattle. // ②You have found / the following blog post. //

③Hello from Seattle! // ④Oct 5, 2020 //

⑤I stopped for coffee / at a café. // ⑥This was an iced coffee / served there. //

⑦Look at the straw. // ⑧It was made of paper, / not plastic! //

⑨At first, / I was a bit afraid / that it would soon get wet and soft, / but there was no problem / at all. // ⑩The paper straw / was actually very strong. // ⑪I felt no difference / from a plastic straw! //

⑫Why didn't the café use / plastic straws? // ⑬Seattle hopes to reduce / plastic waste. // ⑭The city / has now made local food service businesses / stop using plastic straws, / spoons, / forks / and knives. // ⑮They can't provide them / to customers / anymore. // ⑯Instead, / they have to use / something eco-friendly. // ⑰Paper straws are good / for this purpose. //

⑱In addition, / paper straws can have many different designs. // ⑲They can be printed / with a variety of colors and letters. // ⑳Companies can use them / for their advertisements. // ㉑I don't think / this is easy / with plastic straws. //

㉒Paper straws are eco-friendly / and really useful. // ㉓I hope / more will be used / in other places / in the future. //

🔊意味のまとまりに注意して，本文全体を音読しよう。(188 Words)

Words and Phrases	新出単語・表現の意味を調べよう		
blog 图[blɔ́:g] B1	1.	Seattle [siǽt(ə)l]	シアトル
iced 形[áɪst]	2.	straw 图[strɔ́:] B1	3.
be made of …	4.	bit 图[bít] A2	5.
spoon 图[spúːn] A2	6.	provide A to B	7.
eco-friendly 形 [ì:koʊfrén(d)li]	8.		

A 【**Comprehension 1**】 Fill in the blanks in Japanese.

要点を整理しよう【思考力・判断力・表現力】

	紙のストロー	プラスチックのストロー
筆者の感想	使用した感じは（1.　　　　　　　　）。	
シアトル		（2.　　　　　　　　　　　） の削減のため，地域の飲食関係企業での使用を（3.　　　　） した。
企業	簡単に色や文字が印刷できることを活かし，（4.　　　） に利用できる。	

B 【**Comprehension 2**】 Answer the following questions in English.

本文のポイントについて答えよう【思考力・判断力・表現力】

1. What did the person who wrote this blog use at a café in Seattle?

- -

2. What has Seattle made local food service businesses stop doing?

- -

3. Which straws can be printed with colors and letters, plastic ones or paper ones?

- -

C 【**Key Sentences**】 Fill in the blanks and translate the following sentences.

重要文について確認しよう【知識・技能】【思考力・判断力・表現力】

⑨ At first, I was a bit afraid that **it** would soon get wet and soft, but there was no problem at all.

◆ it＝（1.　　　　　　　[日本語で]）。

◆ get … 「… （の状態） になる」。

◆ at all は否定文で，「まったく （…でない)」。

訳 : -

⑭ The city has now **made** local food service businesses **stop** using plastic straws, spoons, forks and knives.

◆ The city＝（2.　　　　　　　[英語で]）。

◆ make は使役動詞で，make＋O＋C（＝原型不定詞） の形で 「O に～させる」 の意味。

◆ stop ～ing は 「～するのをやめる」。

訳 : -

㉓ I hope more will be used in other places in the future.

◆ hope の目的語は more … in the future。that が省略されている。

◆ more＝more （3.　　　　　　　　　[英語2語で]）。

訳 : -

Part 2　教科書 p.106　◀意味のまとまりに注意して，本文全体を聞こう。　◎2-14

①Plastics have made / our lives more convenient, / but plastic waste is / now a global problem / and is getting more and more serious. //

① ②Our lives largely depend on plastics. // ③They are used / for many everyday goods: / shopping bags, / office supplies / and even clothes. // ④From 1950 to 2015, / about 8.3 billion tons of plastics / were created. // ⑤About half of that amount / was produced / in the last 13 years / of that period, / and people are producing / more and more plastics / every year. //

② ⑥What happens / after we throw plastics away? // ⑦Some are burned / as garbage, / but most end up / as waste / in landfills / or in the natural environment. // ⑧In 2015, / the amount of plastic garbage / around the world / reached about 6.3 billion tons. // ⑨Such plastic waste can escape / from the land / into the ocean. // ⑩The amount is estimated / to be more than eight million tons / each year. //

③ ⑪However, / that is not the end / of the story. // ⑫Plastics in the sea / never disappear. // ⑬They continue to pollute our water. // ⑭Sunlight and waves / break them down / into smaller pieces. // ⑮In addition, / dangerous materials / stick to these microplastics / in the environment. // ⑯These plastic bits remain / in the places / where many food sources are found. // ⑰They can be eaten or swallowed / by sea life. //

◀意味のまとまりに注意して，本文全体を音読しよう。(206 Words)

Words and Phrases 新出単語・表現の意味を調べよう			
depend 動[dɪpénd] A2	1.	depend on …	2.
supply 名[səplάɪ] B1	3.	ton 名[tʌ́n] B2	4.
amount 名[əmάʊnt] B1	5.	throw … away	6.
end up in …	7.	landfill 名[lǽndfìl]	8.
estimate 動[éstɪmèɪt] B1	9.	pollute 動[pəlúːt] A2	10.

break A down into B	11.	stick to ...	12.
microplastic 名 [mài krouplǽstɪk]	13.	remain 動 [rɪméɪn] A2	14.
source 名 [sɔ́ːrs] A2	15.	swallow 動 [swá(ː)loʊ] A2	16.

A 【Comprehension 1】 Fill in the blanks in Japanese.

パラグラフごとの要点を整理しよう【思考力・判断力・表現力】

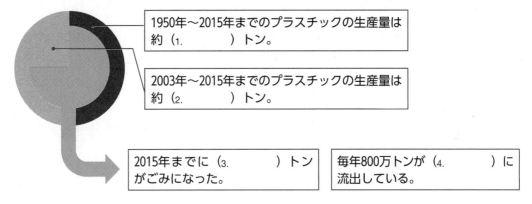

1950年〜2015年までのプラスチックの生産量は約（1.　　　）トン。

2003年〜2015年までのプラスチックの生産量は約（2.　　　）トン。

2015年までに（3.　　　）トンがごみになった。

毎年800万トンが（4.　　　）に流出している。

B 【Comprehension 2】 Answer the following questions in English.

本文のポイントについて答えよう【思考力・判断力・表現力】

1. How much plastic waste is flowing into the sea each year?

---

2. What breaks the plastic in the sea down into smaller pieces?

C 【Key Sentences】 Fill in the blanks and translate the following sentences.

重要文について確認しよう【知識・技能】【思考力・判断力・表現力】

② Our lives largely depend on plastics.

◆ Part 2の主題文である。このプラスチックへの「依存」から派生してくる問題が以降の文で展開される。

訳：

---

⑯ These plastic bits remain in the places (**where** many food sources are found).

◆ where は場所を表す the places を先行詞とする関係副詞である。These plastic bits remain in the places. Many food sources are found there. の there を関係副詞 where を使って1文としたものと考えられる。

訳：

Part 3 教科書 p.107 ◖意味のまとまりに注意して，本文全体を聞こう。 ◎2-16

4 ①In Costa Rica, / a biologist tries / to pull out a plastic straw / from a sea turtle's nose. // ②The turtle is bleeding, / and it appears to be / in a lot of pain. // ③Perhaps it ate the straw / by mistake / and then tried / to throw it up. // ④Instead of getting out of its mouth, / the straw went into its nose. //

5 ⑤Sea animals, / including fish and shellfish, / can mistake plastics / for food / and swallow them. // ⑥The chances are higher / for microplastic pieces. // ⑦The animals cannot digest plastics / in their stomachs, / and they feel full / all the time. // ⑧This makes it difficult / for them / to eat actual food. // ⑨As a result, / many animals in the sea / are dying of starvation. //

6 ⑩We humans / can also be influenced / by plastics / in the sea. // ⑪Scientists believe / that microplastics are present / in seafood. // ⑫Most of them / seem to remain / in the guts / of fish and shellfish. // ⑬It appears / that they do not move / into the parts / we eat. // ⑭However, / the possible risks / to food safety and our health / are still not known. //

◖意味のまとまりに注意して，本文全体を音読しよう。(174 Words)

Words and Phrases	新出単語・表現の意味を調べよう		
Costa Rica [kòustərí:kə]	1.	biologist 名 [baɪá(:)lədʒɪst]	2.
pull out A from B	3.	bleed 動 [blí:d] B1	4.
by mistake	5.	throw … up	6.
go into …	7.	shellfish 名 [ʃélfiʃ]	8.
mistake A for B	9.	digest 動 [daɪdʒést]	10.
all the time	11.	die of …	12.
starvation 名 [stɑːrvéɪʃ(ə)n] B2	13.	gut 名 [gʌ́t] B2	14.
risk 名 [rísk] B1	15.		

A 【**Comprehension 1**】 Fill in the blanks in Japanese.

パラグラフごとの要点を整理しよう【思考力・判断力・表現力】

①プラスチック
ごみは海中で
(1.　　　　　　)
になる。

②(2.　　　　)や
貝や海洋動物
がそれを飲み
込む。

③魚はそれを
(3.　　　　　)
できず満腹を
感じる。
➡(4.　　　　　)
する。

魚を食べる人間に
とっても，健康へ
のリスクがある可
能性がある。

B 【**Comprehension 2**】 Answer the following questions in English.

本文のポイントについて答えよう【思考力・判断力・表現力】

1. What did the biologist try to pull out a plastic straw from?

   ----

2. Why do sea animals eat plastics?

   ----

3. Do many scientists understand the risks that microplastics may cause to human body?

C 【**Key Sentences**】 Fill in the blanks and translate the following sentences.

重要文について確認しよう【知識・技能】【思考力・判断力・表現力】

④ **Instead of** getting out of its mouth, / the straw went into its nose.

◆主節は後半部分である。

◆instead of ... は「(1.　　　　[日本語で])」の意味。

訳 : ---

⑧ This makes **it** difficult for them to eat actual food.

◆This は (2.　　　　　　　　　　　　[日本語で]) ということを指す。

◆it は形式目的語で，真の目的語は (3.　　　　　　　[英語2語で]) actual food。

◆for them は to-不定詞の意味上の主語である。them＝the (4.　　　　　[英語で])。

訳 : ---

⑬ **It appears that** they do not move into the parts (we eat).

◆It appears that ... は「…のように見える，（どうも）…らしい」の意味。

◆the parts を先行詞とする目的格の関係代名詞が省略されている。

訳 : ---

Part 4 教科書 p.110 ◁意味のまとまりに注意して，本文全体を聞こう。 ◎2-18

7 ①What can we do / to stop plastic pollution? // ②One solution is / to use "biodegradable" plastics. // ③They can break down / into water and carbon dioxide (CO_2) / and finally blend with the environment. // ④However, / they may not work / in that way / in dark, cool and low-oxygen places, / such as in the sea. // ⑤For that reason, / biodegradable plastics / may not be the best solution, / although they can be part of it. //

8 ⑥Another solution is recycling. // ⑦Some countries are successful / in promoting it. // ⑧In Norway, / for example, / people can return plastic bottles / to supermarkets / and get a refund / for them. // ⑨This system / has pushed the country's plastic bottle recycling rate / to over 95 percent. // ⑩Across the world, / however, / only 9 percent of used plastics / are recycled. //

9 ⑪What seems important, then, / is cutting the amount / of plastics / we use. // ⑫To achieve this, / many businesses / around the world / are no longer using single-use plastics. // ⑬Plastic-waste control is / not only about / how we should make and recycle plastics. // ⑭It is also about / how we should use plastics. //

◁意味のまとまりに注意して，本文全体を音読しよう。(170 Words)

Words and Phrases 新出単語・表現の意味を調べよう			
biodegradable 形 [bàɪoʊdɪgréɪdəb(ə)l]	1.	carbon 名 [kάːrb(ə)n] B2	2.
dioxide 名 [daɪά(ː)ksaɪd] B1	3.	blend 動 [blénd] B1	4.
blend with ...	5.	oxygen 名 [ά(ː)ksɪdʒ(ə)n] B1	6.
be successful in ...	7.	promote 動 [prəmóʊt] B1	8.
refund 名 [ríːfʌnd] B1	9.	push A to B	10.
no longer	11.	single-use 形 [sìŋgljúːs]	12.

A 【Comprehension 1】 Fill in the blanks in Japanese.

パラグラフごとの要点を整理しよう【思考力・判断力・表現力】

プラスチック汚染防止の方法		
①プラスチックの代わりに（1.　　　）のプラスチックを使う	②プラスチックの（3.　　　　）	③プラスチック使用量の（5.　　　）
⬇	⬇	⬇
（2.　　　　）の解決策ではないかもしれない。	ノルウェーの例 ペットボトルをスーパーに返却すると店は客に（4.　　　　）する。	使い捨てプラスチックの使用をやめる企業も増えている。

B 【Comprehension 2】 Answer the following questions in English.

本文のポイントについて答えよう【思考力・判断力・表現力】

1. What has the refund system in Norway brought to the country?

　--

2. What percentage is the recycling rate of used plastics in the world?

　--

3. What are the three solutions to stop plastic pollution?

　--

C 【Key Sentences】 Fill in the blanks and translate the following sentences.

重要文について確認しよう【知識・技能】【思考力・判断力・表現力】

⑤ For that reason, / biodegradable plastics may not be the best solution, / although they can be part of it.

　◆that は前文を受ける。（1.　　　　　　　　　　　　　　　　[日本語で]）という理由。

　◆they＝（2.　　　　　　[英語 2 語で]），it＝（3.　　　　　[英語で]）

　◆can は可能性を表す。

　訳：--

⑥ Another solution is recycling.

　◆Another は前のパラグラフの One solution を受けている。この文がこのパラグラフの主題文である。

　◆S＋V＋C の文型で，この recycling は「再（生）利用」の意味の名詞で補語となっている。

　訳：--

⑪ What seems important, then, is cutting the amount of plastics (we use).

　◆S＋V＋C の文型。関係代名詞 what の節が全体の主語となり，cutting は動名詞で補語となっている。目的格の関係代名詞が省略されている。

　訳：--

Activity Plus 教科書 p.114〜p.115 🔊意味のまとまりに注意して，本文全体を聞こう。 🎧2-20

①You are doing some research / on the plastic-waste problem. // ②On the Internet, / you have found an article / about a discovery / made by a group of scientists. //

③Can Plastic-Eating Bacteria Save the Earth? //

④Back in 2016, / "PET-eating" bacteria were found. // ⑤PET is a plastic / widely used / in drink bottles. // ⑥Now a group of scientists / has developed a new enzyme / from the bacteria. // ⑦It can break PET down / more quickly. // ⑧While PET takes hundreds of years / to break down / in nature, / the enzyme, / called PETase, / can start the process / in just a few days. //

⑨The discovery came / by chance / when the scientists were looking / into the enzyme. // ⑩They found / that the performance of PETase / could be improved / by changing its surface structure. // ⑪The improved enzyme / was also tested / on another plastic, PEF. // ⑫This plastic is also slow / to break down / in nature. // ⑬The result was surprising. // ⑭The enzyme worked better / on PEF / than on PET. // ⑮The scientists are now trying / to make the enzyme work / even better. // ⑯They hope / that future varieties can work / on other kinds / of plastics. //

⑰PETase could be a solution / to the problem / of recycling plastics. // ⑱Plastic materials lose some quality / each time they are recycled. // ⑲Bottles become clothes, / then carpets, / and finally, waste. // ⑳The recycling circle is not closed. // ㉑However, / PETase may be able to close the circle. // ㉒It can turn plastics / back into their original materials. // ㉓Thanks to this, / plastics may be used / again and again / without losing quality. // ㉔Although this technology hasn't reached practical use yet, / it may give us a hint / about how to solve the plastic-waste problem. // 🔊意味のまとまりに注意して，本文全体を音読しよう。(264 Words)

Words and Phrases 新出単語・表現の意味を調べよう			
discovery 名 [dɪskʌ́v(ə)ri] B1	1.	bacteria 名 [bæktíəriə]	2.
enzyme 名 [énzaɪm]	3.	hundreds of …	4.

PETase [píːiːtíːéɪs]	ペターゼ	process 图[prá(ː)ses] B1	5.
by chance	6.	look into …	7.
surface 形[sə́ːrfəs]	8.	structure 图[strʌ́ktʃər] A2	9.
test A on B	10.	work on …	11.
each time …	12.	turn A back into B	13.
again and again	14.	practical 形 [prǽktɪk(ə)l] B1	15.

A 【Comprehension 1】 Fill in the blanks in Japanese.

要点を整理しよう【思考力・判断力・表現力】

2016年，科学者が PET を食べる（1.　　　　）を発見した。

▼

そこから新しい（2.　　　　）を開発し，それをペターゼと呼んだ。
PET だけでなく，PEF にも効果を発揮した。
ほかのプラスチックにも応用できる可能性がある。

▼

プラスチックを元の材料に戻すことが可能なため，
プラスチックの（3.　　　　）の問題の
解決策になる可能性がある。

（4.　　　　）が
低下し，最終的
にはごみになる。

B 【Comprehension 2】 Answer the following questions in English.

本文のポイントについて答えよう【思考力・判断力・表現力】

1. What is the new enzyme called?

-----

2. Which side did the enzyme work better, on PET or on PEF?

C 【Key Sentence】 Translate the following sentence.

重要文について確認しよう【知識・技能】【思考力・判断力・表現力】

⑮ The scientists are now trying to <u>make</u> the enzyme <u>work</u> even better.
　　　　　　　　　　　　　　　　　　　V　　　　　O　　　　　C

◆ try to ～の後は V（使役動詞）＋O＋C（＝原形不定詞）の文型が使われている。
◆ even は比較級 better を強調している。

訳 : -----

Part 1　教科書 p.120~p.121　◁意味のまとまりに注意して，本文全体を聞こう。　◎2-22

① You are walking / on a street. // ② You find a poster / of an interesting event. //

③ The International Center in Tokyo / will host a special talk. //

④ Living with Hiroshima: My Memories //

⑤ Koko Kondo was born / in Hiroshima / in 1944. // ⑥ She experienced the atomic bombing / when she was just eight months old. // ⑦ After she grew up, / Koko became a storyteller. // ⑧ She has shared her own experiences / with a lot of people, / from small children / to older people. // ⑨ She gives her talks / both in Japanese / and in English. // ⑩ She has received many prizes / for her excellent work / as a peace advocate. //

⑪ 1:30 p.m. on Saturday, July 2, 2022 //

⑫ ◆ Building K, Room 303 //　　⑬ ◆ Admission Free //

⑭ ◆ Information: 0123-45-xxxx //　　⑮ https://www.ictokyo.ac.jp/peace //

⑯ About the Talk //

⑰ After World War II, / Koko remained angry / with those who destroyed Hiroshima. // ⑱ However, / a chance to see an American man / changed her life. // ⑲ He was the co-pilot / of the plane / that dropped the atomic bomb / on Hiroshima. // ⑳ When she saw his deep regret, / Koko realized / what she really hated / was not the person / in front of her / but war itself. // ㉑ Her story gives us a chance / to reflect on our thoughts / about war. //

◁意味のまとまりに注意して，本文全体を音読しよう。(192 Words)

Words and Phrases　新出単語・表現の意味を調べよう			
storyteller 名 [stɔ́:ritèlər] B1	1.	advocate 名 [ǽdvəkət]	2.
admission 名 [ədmíʃ(ə)n] B1	3.	be angry with …	4.
destroy 動 [dɪstrɔ́ɪ] A2	5.	co-pilot 名 [kóupàɪlət]	6.
regret 名 [rɪgrét] B2	7.	not A but B	8.
reflect on …	9.		

A 【Comprehension 1】 Fill in the blanks in Japanese.

要点を整理しよう【思考力・判断力・表現力】

トークイベント			
タイトル	広島とともに生きる：私の記憶	日時	2022年7月2日（土）1：30から
語り手	近藤紘子	場所	東京国際センター
近藤紘子	1944年広島生まれ。生後8か月のときに（1.　　　　）を経験し，その体験を共有する語り部になる。（2.　　　　）と日本語で語る彼女に多くの賞が与えられている。		
話の内容	第二次世界大戦後，広島を（3.　　　　）した人を恨んでいたが，1人のアメリカ人に出会ったことが彼女の（4.　　　　）を変えた。		

B 【Comprehension 2】 Answer the following questions in English.

本文のポイントについて答えよう【思考力・判断力・表現力】

1. How much do you have to pay for the special talk?

   ----

2. What did Koko Kondo become after she grew up?

   ----

3. What did Koko realize when she saw the deep regret of the co-pilot?

C 【Key Sentences】 Fill in the blank and translate the following sentences.

重要文について確認しよう【知識・技能】【思考力・判断力・表現力】

⑰ Koko <u>remained</u> <u>angry</u> with those who destroyed Hiroshima.
   V   C

 ◆ remain は補語をともなう動詞で，S＋V＋C の文である。

 ◆ those who 〜は「(1.　　　　　 [日本語で])」の意味。

 訳：--

⑳ Koko <u>realized</u> <u>what she really hated was not the person in front of her but</u>
    V   O

 <u>war itself</u>.

 ◆ what she really hated was ... 「彼女が本当に憎んでいたことは…」という節が realized の目的語になっている。

 ◆ not A but B の A には the person ..., B には war itself が入る。

 訳：--

㉑ Her story gives us <u>a chance</u> (to reflect on our thoughts about war).

 ◆ a chance はどんな機会かを，直後の to-不定詞が説明している。

 訳：--

Part 2　教科書 p.122　🔊意味のまとまりに注意して，本文全体を聞こう。◎2-24

①Why do the *hibakusha* talk / about the war? // ②What can we learn / from them? // ③What stories need to be passed on / to the next generations? //

① ④Two atomic bombs were dropped / on Japan / in August 1945. // ⑤About 140,000 people / in Hiroshima / and about 70,000 people / in Nagasaki / had died / by the end of the year. // ⑥Seventy-one years later, / in May 2016, / Barack Obama became the first sitting president / to visit Hiroshima. // ⑦He made a speech there / and told the world / the importance / of giving up nuclear weapons. //

② ⑧In his speech, / President Obama referred to a woman / who had forgiven a pilot / who dropped the atomic bomb / on Hiroshima. // ⑨The woman's name / is Koko Kondo. // ⑩She has shared her story / as a *hibakusha*, / a surviving victim / of the atomic bombings. // ⑪Obama's speech / helped her activities / gain worldwide recognition. //

③ ⑫Koko's father, / Kiyoshi Tanimoto, / was a famous pastor / who also survived the bombing. // ⑬He is one of the main characters / in *Hiroshima*, / a book / written by John Hersey. // ⑭The war left many young women / injured by the atomic bomb. // ⑮Kiyoshi helped them / receive medical care / in the United States. // ⑯He had a great influence / on Koko. // ⑰If he were alive now, / what would he say / to his daughter? //

🔊意味のまとまりに注意して，本文全体を音読しよう。(207 Words)

Words and Phrases	新出単語・表現の意味を調べよう		
pass on A to B	1.	Barack Obama [bərɑ́ːk oʊbɑ́ːmə]	バラク・オバマ
give up ...	2.	nuclear 形 [njúːkliər] B1	3.
weapon 名 [wép(ə)n] B1	4.	refer 動 [rɪfə́ːr] A2	5.
refer to ...	6.	forgiven [fərgív(ə)n]	forgive の過去分詞形

forgive 動 [fərgív] B1	7.	survive 動 [sərváɪv] A2	8.
victim 名 [víktɪm] B1	9.	worldwide 形 [wə́:r(d)wàɪd] B2	10.
recognition 名 [rèkəgníʃ(ə)n] B2	11.	pastor 名 [pǽstər] B2	12.
John Hersey [dʒá(:)n há:rsi]	ジョン・ハーシー	medical 形 [médɪk(ə)l] A2	13.
have an influence on …	14.		

A 【Comprehension 1】 Fill in the blanks in Japanese.

パラグラフごとの要点を整理しよう【思考力・判断力・表現力】

1945年8月 ▶▶▶	2016年5月
<u>原爆投下</u> 広島 　死者：約14万人 長崎 　死者：約7万人	(1.　　　　　　　) が広島訪問し，(2.　　　　　　　) の重要性について演説した。 (3.　　　　) として話をする近藤紘子さんについて言及した。 近藤さんの父である谷本牧師は，ジョン・ハーシーの著書の (4.　　　　) である。

B 【Comprehension 2】 Answer the following questions in English.

本文のポイントについて答えよう【思考力・判断力・表現力】

1. After World War II, did many American presidents visit Hiroshima?

   ----

2. What did Kiyoshi Tanimoto do in the United States?

C 【Key Sentences】 Fill in the blanks and translate the following sentences.

重要文について確認しよう【知識・技能】【思考力・判断力・表現力】

⑧ President Obama referred to a woman (**who** had forgiven a pilot (**who** dropped the atomic bomb on Hiroshima)).

◆a woman who had forgiven a pilot は (1.　　　　　　　[英語2語で]) のことである。
◆関係代名詞の節の中の名詞がさらに関係代名詞によって説明されている。

訳：--

⑰ If he were alive now, what would he say to his daughter?

◆If＋S＋were …, S＋would ～は，「もし（今）…なら，～するだろう」の意味の仮定法過去の文。
◆alive は形容詞で「(2.　　　　　　[日本語で])」の意味。

訳：--

Part 3 教科書 p.124 🔊意味のまとまりに注意して，本文全体を聞こう。 ◉2-26

④ ①Fortunately, / Koko's family survived the bombing, / although they had to face / the terrible realities / of the war. // ②They saw many people / come to their church: / women with terrible burns / on their faces, / children who had lost their families, / and people suffering from the aftereffects / of the bomb. // ③At that time, / Koko couldn't help thinking, / "If the Americans had not dropped / the atomic bomb, / we wouldn't have gone through this terribly painful experience." //

⑤ ④Koko had long wanted / to avenge the victims, / and a chance actually came / when she was ten years old. // ⑤She got the chance / to visit America / and appear on a TV show / featuring her father. // ⑥The program / secretly planned a meeting / between her family and Captain Robert Lewis, / the co-pilot / of the Enola Gay. //

⑥ ⑦At first, / Koko thought / she would kick and bite Lewis, / but the next moment, / she was surprised / to see the pilot's eyes / filled with tears. // ⑧He remembered the bombing / and said, / "My God, / what have we done?" // ⑨He bitterly regretted / carrying out the bombing order. // ⑩In that moment, / Koko realized / the pilot was also a victim / of war. //

🔊意味のまとまりに注意して，本文全体を音読しよう。(184 Words)

Words and Phrases 新出単語・表現の意味を調べよう			
fortunately 副 [fɔ́ːrtʃ(ə)nətli] A2	1.	suffer from ...	2.
aftereffect 名 [ǽftərɪfèkt]	3.	cannot help 〜ing	4.
avenge 動 [əvén(d)ʒ]	5.	secretly 副 [síːkrətli] B1	6.
Robert Lewis [rá(ː)bərt lúːɪs]	ロバート・ルイス	Enola Gay [ɪnóʊlə géɪ]	エノラ・ゲイ
bite 動 [báɪt] B1	7.	the next moment	8.
be filled with ...	9.	bitterly 副 [bítərli] B2	10.

A 【Comprehension 1】 Fill in the blanks in Japanese.

パラグラフごとの要点を整理しよう【思考力・判断力・表現力】

近藤さんの心情の変化

| 原爆投下直後
アメリカ人が原爆を投下し
なかったら，ひどい
(1.　　　　) をすることは
なかったのに，と考えずに
はいられなかった。 | 最初に副操縦士を見たとき
パイロットを (2.　　　　)，
噛んだりしたいと思った。 | 副操縦士の涙を見た後
彼も戦争の (3.　　　　) な
のだと気付いた。 |

B 【Comprehension 2】 Answer the following questions in English.

本文のポイントについて答えよう【思考力・判断力・表現力】

1. Did Koko want to avenge the victims of the atomic bombing before she visited America?

　..

2. Who did the TV program feature?

　..

3. When Koko saw the co-pilot's eyes filled with tears, what did she realize?

　..

C 【Key Sentences】 Fill in the blank and translate the following sentences.

重要文について確認しよう【知識・技能】【思考力・判断力・表現力】

② They saw many people come to their church: ...

　◆ see（知覚動詞）＋O＋C（＝動詞の原形）は「O が C するのを見る」の意味。
　◆「:（コロン）」に続く部分は，ここでは many people の内容を具体的に書いている。
　訳：..

③ If the Americans had not dropped the atomic bomb, we wouldn't have gone through this terribly painful experience.

　◆ If＋S＋had＋過去分詞 ...，S＋would have ～は，「もし（過去に）…だったなら，～しただろう」
　　の意味の仮定法過去完了の文。
　◆ this terribly painful experience とは（1.　　　　　　　　　[日本語で]）を見たこと。
　訳：..

⑦ At first, Koko thought she would kick and bite **Lewis**, but the next moment, she was surprised to see **the pilot**'s eyes filled with tears.

　◆ Lewis と the pilot は同一人物で，言いかえられている。
　◆ see（知覚動詞）＋O＋C（＝過去分詞）は「O が C されるのを見る」の意味。
　訳：..

Part 4 教科書 p.125 🔊意味のまとまりに注意して，本文全体を聞こう。 💿2-28

⑦ ①That important event / changed Koko's way / of thinking. // ②She wrote / in her book later, / "If I had not met Captain Robert Lewis, / I might have become a person / who never forgives others." // ③She then began to realize / the necessity / of spreading the memory / of the war / from person to person. // ④This was the beginning / of her lifework / as a storyteller / and peace advocate. //

⑧ ⑤The stories told by the *hibakusha*, / including Koko's, / have been received / in many ways / by younger people. // ⑥Some of them / have also become new storytellers / who hand down the stories / of the *hibakusha*. // ⑦Others try to express / the horrors of war / by painting, / acting / or giving music performances. // ⑧They all believe / that the experiences of the *hibakusha* / need to be shared / with future generations. //

⑨ ⑨Someday, / we will no longer be able to hear / the living voices / of the *hibakusha*. // ⑩However, / the memories of August 6 and 9, 1945, / must never fade away. // ⑪As Japan is the only country / that has ever suffered / atomic bomb attacks, / each of us has a responsibility / to hand down the memories / of the war / to future generations. // ⑫In the future, / how will you share / what you know / about war? // 🔊意味のまとまりに注意して，本文全体を音読しよう。(197 Words)

Words and Phrases 新出単語・表現の意味を調べよう			
necessity 名[nəsésəti] B2	1.	from A to A	2.
lifework 名[làɪfwə́ːrk]	3.	hand down …	4.
horror 名[hɔ́ːrər] A2	5.	fade 動[féɪd] B1	6.
fade away	7.	responsibility 名[rɪspà(ː)nsəbíləti] B1	8.

A 【Comprehension 1】 Fill in the blanks in Japanese.

パラグラフごとの要点を整理しよう【思考力・判断力・表現力】

近藤さんが語り部になった理由	ロバート・ルイスに出会ったことから，戦争の記憶を人から人へと広めていく（1.　　　）に気付いた。
被爆者の話は受け継がれている	（2.　　　）からの話を受け継いで語り部になる人や，絵や演劇や（3.　　　）を通じて戦争の怖さを表現する人もいる。
語り継がれる意義	日本は原爆投下を受けた唯一の国であり，その記憶を次の世代へと語り継いでいく（4.　　　）がある。

B 【Comprehension 2】 Answer the following questions in English.

本文のポイントについて答えよう【思考力・判断力・表現力】

1. Do some of the younger people become new storytellers of war?

　　--

2. What country has ever suffered atomic bomb attacks?

　　--

C 【Key Sentences】 Translate the following sentences.

重要文について確認しよう【知識・技能】【思考力・判断力・表現力】

② If I had not met Captain Robert Lewis, I might have become a person (**who** never forgives others).
  ◆仮定法過去完了の文である。
  ◆関係代名詞 who の先行詞は a person。
  訳：--

⑧ They all believe that the experiences of the *hibakusha* need to be shared with future generations.
  ◆ that-節が目的語にあたる S＋V＋O の文。
  ◆ need to be shared with ...「…に共有される必要がある」。受け身の不定詞は〈to be＋過去分詞〉となる。
  訳：--

⑪ As Japan is the only country that has ever suffered atomic bomb attacks, / each of us has a responsibility (to hand down the memories of the war to future generations).
  ◆ As は理由を表す節を導いている。
  ◆先行詞（人ではないもの）が the only などをともなっていると，関係代名詞は that を用いることが多い。
  ◆ to hand down ... は a responsibility の内容を説明する to-不定詞の形容詞用法。
  訳：--

Activity Plus 教科書 p.128〜p.129 🔊意味のまとまりに注意して，本文全体を聞こう。 🎧2-30

①You are listening to a discussion / about the definition / of peace. //

Teacher: ②The definition of peace / can differ / among us. // ③A dictionary may define it / as a state or period / without war. // ④If so, / the opposite word / of peace / will be war. // ⑤However, / not all of us / agree with this definition / as we may not feel peaceful / even when we are not fighting / each other. // ⑥How would you define peace? // ⑦Discuss it / in your group. //

Mika: ⑧I define peace / as a state / of having the necessities / for life. // ⑨If we didn't have enough food, / clothing / and housing, / it would be difficult / to live. // ⑩Having the necessities / for life / is the basis / of peace, / I believe. //

Satoshi: ⑪I agree with Mika, / but I also think of peace / as a state / of being safe. // ⑫Nobody wants to have car accidents. // ⑬Nobody wants to be attacked / when they are walking / at night. // ⑭Safety must be part of peace. // ⑮What do you think, Emily? //

Emily: ⑯Um, personally, / I feel peaceful / when I'm having a meal / with my family / or talking / with my friends. // ⑰That is not something special / at all. // ⑱Just being able to spend a normal life / means peace / to me. //

Satoshi: ⑲I like your idea, Emily. // ⑳Although we don't usually notice that, / we may have peace already / in our life. //

🔊意味のまとまりに注意して，本文全体を音読しよう。(213 Words)

Words and Phrases	新出単語・表現の意味を調べよう		
discussion 名 [dɪskʌ́ʃ(ə)n] A2	1.	definition 名 [dèfəníʃ(ə)n] B1	2.
differ 動 [dífər] B1	3.	define 動 [dɪfáɪn] B1	4.
define A as B	5.	opposite 形 [ɑ́(ː)pəzɪt] A2	6.
agree with …	7.	peaceful 形 [píːsf(ə)l] A2	8.
clothing 名 [klóʊðɪŋ] B2	9.	um [ʌ́m]	(間投詞) うーん，いや

82

A 【**Comprehension 1**】 Fill in the blanks in Japanese.

要点を整理しよう【思考力・判断力・表現力】

【平和とは】 生きるのに (1.　　　　　) を 持つこと。 例) 食べ物や衣類, 　　家など。 ミカ	【平和とは】 (2.　　　　　) である こと。 例) 交通事故などに 　　あわない。 サトシ	【平和とは】 (3.　　　　　) の生活 を送ること。 例) 友達と話したり, 　　家族と食事したり 　　する。 エミリー

B 【**Comprehension 2**】 Answer the following questions in English.

本文のポイントについて答えよう【思考力・判断力・表現力】

1. Who thinks that peace is just being able to spend a normal life?

　　--

2. What does Satoshi think of peace as?

　　--

3. Does Satoshi agree with Emily's opinion?

　　--

C 【**Key Sentences**】 Fill in the blanks and translate the following sentences.

重要文について確認しよう【知識・技能】【思考力・判断力・表現力】

③ A dictionary may define it as a state or period without war.
　◆ without ... 「…のない」。
　◆ it = (1.　　　　[英語で])。
　訳：--

⑤ **Not all** of us agree with this definition **as** we may not feel peaceful even when
　we are not fighting each other.
　◆ not all ... は部分否定で,「すべてが…とは限らない」の意味となる。
　◆ as は because の意味で, 理由を表す節が続く。
　訳：--

⑰ That is **not** something special **at all**.
　◆ That は (2.　　　　　　　　　　　[日本語で]) ということ。
　◆ not ... at all は「まったく…ない」の意味。
　訳：--

Part 1 教科書 p.134～p.135 📢意味のまとまりに注意して，本文全体を聞こう。 ◎2-32

① One morning, / you read an advertisement / about a new supermarket. // ② You go there / and then listen to an announcement / at the supermarket. //

③ Welcome to *Amazing Supermarket!* // ④ Now Open in Your Town! //

⑤ A unique new supermarket opens / in your town today! //

・⑥ No need to bring money. //

・⑦ No waiting in line / to pay for your shopping. //

⑧ Come and enjoy shopping / at our first store / in your town! //

⑨ Here is how you shop / at our supermarket: //

1　⑩ Install the *Amazing Supermarket* application / in your smartphone / before you come. //

2　⑪ Bring your smartphone with you / instead of money. //

3　⑫ Enter *Amazing Supermarket*. // ⑬ Touch your smartphone / on the reader / at the entrance. //

4　⑭ Start your shopping. // ⑮ Put the items you want / into your shopping bag. // ⑯ You can return them / to their original places / if you change your mind. //

5　⑰ Go back to the entrance / where you came in, / and just walk out / with the items. //

6　⑱ Check your smartphone / after shopping. // ⑲ Your receipt will arrive soon / after you leave *Amazing Supermarket*. //

⑳ For more information, / please contact us: / https://www.amazingsupermarket.com //

㉑ Tel.: 888-550-xxxx // ㉒ Visit our first shop / at 8th Street, / Washington St. 22885. //

㉓ Good morning, customers. // ㉔ Thank you very much / for visiting *Amazing Supermarket* / on opening day. // ㉕ Before you start shopping, / just a couple of things / to remember. //

㉖ When you touch your smartphone / on the phone reader, / please make sure / that your *Amazing Supermarket* application / has been started successfully. // ㉗ After you choose an item, / if you decide to return it, / please put it back / in its original place. //

㉘ We're having an opening sale / for one week. // ㉙ All items are 20% off / from our usual price, / so don't miss this chance! // ㉚ Enjoy your shopping! //

📢意味のまとまりに注意して，本文全体を音読しよう。(279 Words)

Words and Phrases	新出単語・表現の意味を調べよう		
in line	1.	pay for …	2.
install 動[ɪnstɔ́ːl] B1	3.	receipt 图[rɪsíːt] A2	4.
a couple of …	5.	make sure that …	6.

A【Comprehension 1】 Fill in the blanks in Japanese.

要点を整理しよう【思考力・判断力・表現力】

Amazing Supermarket の特徴
・お金を持って行く必要がない。　・買い物の支払いに（1.　　　）必要がない。
Amazing Supermarket での買い物の手順
店のアプリケーションを（2.　　　　）したスマートフォンを入り口のリーダーにタッチし，ほしい商品を買い物袋に入れ，店を出る。するとスマートフォンに（3.　　　）が届く。
店内アナウンスより

・（4.　　　）が起動されたことを確認してください。
・選んだ商品を返す場合は，（5.　　　）に戻してください。
・オープニングセールは（6.　　　）開催する予定です。
・全商品（7.　　　）％割引です。

B【Comprehension 2】 Answer the following questions in English.

本文のポイントについて答えよう【思考力・判断力・表現力】

1. What do you have to do before you go to the supermarket?

2. What will happen when you check your smartphone after shopping?

C【Key Sentences】 Fill in the blanks and translate the following sentences.

重要文について確認しよう【知識・技能】【思考力・判断力・表現力】

⑦ No waiting in line / to pay for your shopping.
　◆No ～ing「～しない」はキャッチコピーなどによく使われる表現。
　◆to pay for … は waiting in line を修飾する to-不定詞の副詞用法で，目的を表す。
　訳：

⑰ Go back to the entrance (**where** you came in), and just walk out with the items.
　◆where は関係副詞で，先行詞は the entrance。
　訳：

Part 2 教科書 p.136〜p.137 ◀意味のまとまりに注意して，本文全体を聞こう。 ◎2-34

①AI, or artificial intelligence, / is one of the hottest topics / in our society today. //
②Have you ever used AI technology? // ③Have you ever been to places / where AI technology is used? //

1 ④You see a colorful advertisement / in your morning newspaper. // ⑤While you are looking it over, / your eyes stop / on this sentence: / "No waiting in line / to pay for your shopping." // ⑥Getting interested in this new store, / you decide / to buy some things there. //

2 ⑦Before you go to *Amazing Supermarket*, / you need to download an application / onto your smartphone. // ⑧This is necessary / in order to create your account / and allow cashless shopping / in the store. // ⑨When you arrive / at the supermarket, / you need to touch your smartphone / on the phone reader / at the entrance. // ⑩Then your shopping record becomes active / and you are ready / to do your shopping. //

3 ⑪Although you may not notice, / while you are shopping, / many small cameras and sensors / which have different purposes / are tracking you / all over the store. // ⑫These devices sense the items / you pick up / and automatically add them / to your smartphone shopping list. // ⑬Meanwhile, / any item you return / to its shelf / is removed / from the list. // ⑭You think, / "I understand! // ⑮This is AI!" // ⑯You have just remembered the news / you heard / a few days ago. // ⑰"AI is operating this store," / the news said. //

◀意味のまとまりに注意して，本文全体を音読しよう。(220 Words)

Words and Phrases	新出単語・表現の意味を調べよう		
artificial 形 [à:rtɪfíʃ(ə)l] A2	1.	intelligence 名 [ɪntélɪdʒ(ə)ns] A2	2.
look over ...	3.	download 動 [dáʊnlòʊd] A2	4.
onto 前 [á(:)ntə] B1	5.	account 名 [əkáʊnt] A2	6.
allow 動 [əláʊ] A2	7.	cashless 形 [kǽʃləs]	8.

be ready to ～	9.	sensor 名[sénsər]	10.
pick up ...	11.	meanwhile 副 [mí:n(h)wàɪl] B1	12.
remove 動[rɪmú:v] B1	13.		

A 【Comprehension 1】 Fill in the blanks in Japanese.

パラグラフごとの要点を整理しよう【思考力・判断力・表現力】

朝刊の広告で「買い物の支払いに並ぶ必要はありません。」という言葉が目に留まり，その店に興味を持ち，そこで何かを買うことにする。

買い物の前にアプリケーションをスマートフォンに（1.　　　）し，（2.　　　）を作成する。店の入り口でスマートフォンをリーダーにタッチし，買い物の履歴が起動する。

買い物中
たくさんのカメラやセンサーが客を追尾し，客が（3.　　　）商品をスマートフォンのリストに自動で追加する。商品を元に戻すとリストから（4.　　　）される。

B 【Comprehension 2】 Answer the following questions in English.

本文のポイントについて答えよう【思考力・判断力・表現力】

1. What do you need to do when you arrive at the supermarket?

---

2. What do the devices tracking you all over the store do?

C 【Key Sentences】 Fill in the blank and translate the following sentences.

重要文について確認しよう【知識・技能】【思考力・判断力・表現力】

④ You see a colorful advertisement in your morning newspaper.

◆状況の描写や説明などで，読み手に実感をもって伝わるようにするために，読み手の視点で主語は you を用い，動詞は現在形にすることで，あたかも読み手がその場にいるかのように表現している。

訳 : ---

⑥ **Getting** interested in this new store, / you decide to buy some things there.

◆分詞構文は，分詞で始まる句が「時」や「理由」などの意味を表す。分詞の主語と時は主節に一致する。Getting interested in ... の意味上の主語は（1.　　　[英語で]）である。

◆ get interested in ... 「…に興味を持つ」

訳 : ---

87

Part 3 教科書 p.138 ◁意味のまとまりに注意して，本文全体を聞こう。 ◎2-36

④ ①AI was created / after World War II / by a number of scientists, / and it has been introduced / into a variety of fields today. // ②Some fields are basic, / while others are more advanced. //

⑤ ③Image recognition, / such as telling apples / from oranges, / is one example. // ④First, / the AI needs to learn / just as we humans do. // ⑤A number of apple and orange images / are delivered / to the AI. // ⑥When the AI is given a "viewpoint," / such as "color," / to distinguish the apples / from the oranges, / then it learns / to do so / even with new incoming apple and orange images. // ⑦This stage of learning / is called "machine learning." // ⑧At the more advanced stage / called "deep learning," / the AI learns / to find viewpoints / by itself. // ⑨This is based on / a large amount of information / from outside. // ⑩The AI then learns / how to search for subtle information / about apples, / such as their size, / shape / or quality, / to separate them / without any instruction / from human beings. //

⑥ ⑪Deep learning / is an essential part / of AI / because it has made AI / different from a simple automation tool. // ⑫With deep learning, / AI can usually make the best decision, / just as we humans do / in our everyday lives. //

◁意味のまとまりに注意して，本文全体を音読しよう。(198 Words)

Words and Phrases　新出単語・表現の意味を調べよう			
a number of …	1.	advanced 形[ədvǽnst] A2	2.
tell [distinguish] A from B	3.	viewpoint 名[vjúːpɔ̀ɪnt] B1	4.
distinguish 動 [dɪstíŋgwɪʃ] B1	5.	learn to ～	6.
incoming 形[ínkʌ̀mɪŋ]	7.	by oneself	8.
be based on …	9.	subtle 形[sʌ́t(ə)l] B2	10.
instruction 名 [ɪnstrʌ́kʃ(ə)n] B1	11.	automation 名 [ɔ̀ːtəméɪʃ(ə)n]	12.

A 【Comprehension 1】 Fill in the blanks in Japanese.

パラグラフごとの要点を整理しよう【思考力・判断力・表現力】

> AI は（1.　　　　　　　　　　　　　　　　）後に生み出され，さまざまな分野に導入されている。
> 例）リンゴとオレンジを区別するような（2.　　　　）認識。

機械学習
AI には「色」のような「観点（特徴量）」を人間から与えられ物を識別する。

深層学習（ディープラーニング）
AI は「観点（特徴量）」を AI 自身で見つける。

> AI は人間が日常生活でするのと同じように最善の（3.　　　　）ができる。

B 【Comprehension 2】 Answer the following questions in English.

本文のポイントについて答えよう【思考力・判断力・表現力】

1. What makes it possible for the AI to tell the apples from the oranges?

2. What does the AI learn at the "deep learning" stage?

3. Why is deep learning an essential part of AI?

C 【Key Sentences】 Fill in the blanks and translate the following sentences.

重要文について確認しよう【知識・技能】【思考力・判断力・表現力】

⑤ A number of apple and orange images are delivered to the AI.

　◆事実や情報の詳細を客観的に説明する場合，主語に特定の人物を置かずに受動態を使う。

　訳：

⑥ When the AI is given a "viewpoint," such as "color," to distinguish the apples from the oranges, then **it** learns to **do so** even with new incoming apple and orange images.

　◆ it＝（1.　　　[英語で]），do so＝（2.　　　　　　[日本語で]）

　訳：

⑩ The AI then learns how to search for subtle information about apples, such as their size, shape or quality, to separate them without any instruction from human beings.

　◆ such as their size, shape or quality は subtle information「かすかな情報」の具体例。
　◆ to separate them は目的を表す to-不定詞の副詞用法。them＝（3.　　　　　[英語で]）。

　訳：

Part 4 教科書 p.140 ◀意味のまとまりに注意して，本文全体を聞こう。◎2-38

7 ①After your new experience / at *Amazing Supermarket*, / a worry spreads / in your mind: / "In the future, / will AI take over jobs / from human beings?" // ②To answer this question, / you need to think / about what AI is better at doing / than human beings / and what you can do better / than AI. //

8 ③It is true / that AI is better than you / when it comes to searching / for information / from a huge amount of data / and making the best decision. // ④However, / you have abilities / which are unique / to human beings. // ⑤You can create new ideas, / and you can love / things and people. //

9 ⑥Artists and inventors are creative. // ⑦On this point, / AI can never replace them. // ⑧Doctors, / childcare workers / and teachers / need to feel love / toward the people / they interact with / in their jobs. // ⑨AI, which lacks this feeling, / cannot do these types / of jobs. //

10 ⑩AI has huge potential / to make our future brighter. // ⑪It is our responsibility / to create a good society / where human beings and AI / can go hand in hand together. // ◀意味のまとまりに注意して，本文全体を音読しよう。(170 Words)

Words and Phrases 新出単語・表現の意味を調べよう			
inventor 名 [ɪnvéntər] B2	1.	creative 形 [kriéɪtɪv] A2	2.
replace 動 [rɪpléɪs] A2	3.	childcare 名 [tʃáɪldkèər]	4.
interact 動 [ìnt(ə)rǽkt] B1	5.	interact with …	6.
lack 動 [lǽk] A2	7.	potential 名 [pəténʃ(ə)l] B1	8.
hand in hand	9.		

A 【Comprehension 1】 Fill in the blanks in Japanese.

パラグラフごとの要点を整理しよう【思考力・判断力・表現力】

AI の普及でわき上がる疑問
AI は人間から (1.   )
を奪ってしまうのではないか。

AI ができること
大量のデータから
(2.   ) を探し,
最善の決定ができる。

人間ができること
新しいアイディアの
(3.   )。
物や人を (4.   )
こと。

AI にできない職業
・(5.   ) な仕事：芸術家,発明家
・人とふれ合うことが必要な仕事：医者,(6.   ),教員

B 【Comprehension 2】 Answer the following questions in English.

本文のポイントについて答えよう【思考力・判断力・表現力】

1. What do you worry after you went to *Amazing Supermarket*?

   ----

2. What is AI better at doing than human beings?

   ----

3. Considering that AI has huge potential to make our future brighter, what do we have to do?

C 【Key Sentences】 Fill in the blanks and translate the following sentences.

重要文について確認しよう【知識・技能】【思考力・判断力・表現力】

② To answer this question, / you need to think about $\boxed{\textbf{what} \text{ AI is better at doing than human beings}}$ and $\boxed{\textbf{what} \text{ you can do better than AI}}$.

◆ what の節 2 つが and で並列されており,think about ... の目的語になっている。

◆ this question＝(1.   [日本語で]) という疑問。

訳： --

⑨ AI, (**which** lacks this feeling), cannot do these types of jobs.

◆ , which は非制限用法の関係代名詞。先行詞の AI に情報を補足して説明している。

◆ these types of jobs＝医者や教員のような (2.   [日本語で]) 職業。

訳： --

⑪ It is our responsibility to create a good society (**where** human beings and AI can go hand in hand together).

◆ It は形式主語で,真主語は to create 以下の内容。

◆ where は関係副詞で,先行詞は a good society。

訳： --

Activity Plus 教科書 p.144~p.145 ◁意味のまとまりに注意して，本文全体を聞こう。 ◎2-40

① You are at a special exhibition / about AI. // ② In front of you / there are four exhibition sections / for different fields. // ③ You are learning / about the latest AI applications / in each field. //

④ Transportation // ⑤ Can you imagine / all the members / of your family / playing cards, / eating lunch, / or watching videos / while your family car drives you / to your travel goal? // ⑥ No one is driving the car, / but AI is! // ⑦ This is no longer a dream. // ⑧ Some companies are expecting / completely self-driving AI cars / in the near future. //

⑨ Communication // ⑩ Perhaps you have heard such words / as "audio recognition" and "machine translation." // ⑪ These technologies became possible / through deep-learning AI. // ⑫ Your foreign language skills / can be supported / by these technologies / when you need to communicate / with people / in different countries, / particularly for such events / as business meetings or traveling abroad. //

⑬ Healthcare // ⑭ AI makes medical tools and medical care / much smarter / and more patient-specific. // ⑮ AI collects data / from many sources / and combines it / with big data. // ⑯ Doctors can use the data / to give faster and better care. // ⑰ Elderly patients / at many nursing homes / don't have to go / to the hospital anymore. //

⑱ Agriculture // ⑲ Agriculture is an industry / where AI is used widely. // ⑳ AI plays three main important roles; / operating small flying machines / to take care of farming products, / monitoring soil conditions, / and estimating farming environments / to decide on the best moment / for planting and harvesting. //

◁意味のまとまりに注意して，本文全体を音読しよう。(228 Words)

Words and Phrases　新出単語・表現の意味を調べよう

transportation 名 [trænspərtéɪʃ(ə)n] B1	1.	drive A to B	2.
completely 副 [kəmplíːtli] B1	3.	self-driving 形 [sèlfdráɪvɪŋ]	4.
audio 形 [ɔ́ːdiòʊ] A2	5.	translation 名 [trænsléɪʃ(ə)n] B2	6.
particularly 副 [pərtíkjələrli] B1	7.	healthcare 名 [hélθkèər] B2	8.

specific 形[spəsífɪk] A2	9.	combine A with B	10.
agriculture 名 [ǽgrɪkʌltʃər] B1	11.	industry 名[índəstri] B1	12.
soil 名[sɔ́ɪl] B2	13.	harvest 動[háːrvɪst] A2	14.

A 【Comprehension 1】 Fill in the blanks in Japanese.

要点を整理しよう【思考力・判断力・表現力】

輸送	コミュニケーション
AI による（1. ）の自動車	（2. ）や（3. ）による外国人との意思疎通サポート

― AI に関する特別展で紹介された AI 技術 ―

医療・保健	農業
はるかに洗練され，よりいっそう患者に特化した医療機器とケア	（4. ）を使った農作物の世話，（5. ）の状態の観察，植え付けや収穫に最良のタイミングを見極める農作業環境の評価

B 【Comprehension 2】 Answer the following questions in English.

本文のポイントについて答えよう【思考力・判断力・表現力】

1. What are some automobile companies expecting in the near future?

---

2. What can doctors use to give faster and better care?

C 【Key Sentences】 Fill in the blank and translate the following sentences.

重要文について確認しよう【知識・技能】【思考力・判断力・表現力】

⑤ Can you <u>imagine</u> <u>all the members of your family</u> <u>playing cards</u>, <u>eating lunch</u>, or <u>watching videos</u> / while your family car drives you to your travel goal?
    （imagine の上に V、all the members of your family の上に O）
◆imagine＋O＋〜ing は「O が〜するのを想像する」の意味。
訳：

⑥ No one is driving the car, but AI is!
◆no one＝nobody「（人間が）だれも…ない」の意味。単数扱い。
◆AI is の後に（1. ［英語で］）the car が省略されている。
訳：

93

Part 1 教科書 p.150〜p.151 ◁意味のまとまりに注意して，本文全体を聞こう。◎2-42

①Jimmy Valentine was released / from prison, / and it was just a week later / that a safe was broken open / in Richmond, / Indiana. // ②Eight hundred dollars was stolen. // ③Two weeks after that, / a safe / in Logansport / was opened, / and fifteen hundred dollars / was taken. // ④Everyone was shocked, / as this safe was so strong / that people thought / no one could break it open. // ⑤Then / a safe / in Jefferson City / was opened, / and five thousand dollars / was stolen. //

⑥Ben Price was a detective. // ⑦He was a big man, / and famous for his skill / at solving very difficult and important cases. // ⑧So now / he began / to work on these three cases. // ⑨He was the only person / who knew / how Jimmy did his job. // ⑩People / with safes / full of money / were glad / to hear / that Ben Price was at work / trying to arrest Mr. Valentine. //

⑪One afternoon, / Jimmy Valentine and his suitcase / arrived in a small town / named Elmore. // ⑫Jimmy, / looking like an athletic young man / just home from college, / walked down the street / toward the hotel. //

⑬A young lady walked / across the street, / passed him / at the corner, / and went through a door / with a sign / "The Elmore Bank" / on it. // ⑭Jimmy Valentine looked into her eyes, / forgot at once / what he was, / and became another man. // ⑮The young lady looked back at him, / and then lowered her eyes / as her face became red. // ⑯Handsome young men / like Jimmy / were not often seen / in Elmore. // ◁意味のまとまりに注意して，本文全体を音読しよう。(241 Words)

Words and Phrases 新出単語・表現の意味を調べよう			
Jimmy Valentine [dʒími væləntàɪn]	ジミー・バレンタイン	release A from B	1.
prison 图[príz(ə)n] B1	2.	break ... open	3.
Richmond [rítʃmənd]	リッチモンド	Indiana [ìndiǽnə]	インディアナ州
stolen [stóʊlən]	steal の過去分詞形	steal 動[stíːl] A2	4.
Logansport [lóʊɡənzpɔ̀ːrt]	ローガンズポート	Jefferson City [dʒéfərs(ə)nsíti]	ジェファーソンシティ

Ben Price [bén práis]	ベン・プライス	detective 图[dɪtéktɪv] B1	5.
at work	6.	Elmore [élmɔːr]	エルモア
athletic 形[æθlétɪk] B1	7.	at once	8.
look back at …	9.	lower 動[lóuər] B2	10.

A 【Comprehension 1】 Fill in the blanks in Japanese.

要点を整理しよう【思考力・判断力・表現力】

ジミー・バレンタイン	・(1.　　　　　) を出てから，リッチモンド，ローガンズポート，ジェファーソンシティで（2.　　　　　） をくり返す。 ・(3.　　　　) に到着後，銀行に入っていく若い女性に興味をもつ。
ベン・プライス	・有能な（4.　　　） であり，金庫破りの事件でジミーを追っている。

B 【Comprehension 2】 Answer the following questions in English.

本文のポイントについて答えよう【思考力・判断力・表現力】

1. Had Jimmy Valentine been arrested before he broke open a safe in Richmond?

    ----

2. When Jimmy arrived in Elmore, where did he head for first?

C 【Key Sentences】 Fill in the blanks and translate the following sentences.

重要文について確認しよう【知識・技能】【思考力・判断力・表現力】

⑩ People with safes (full of money) were glad to hear that Ben Price was at work trying to arrest Mr. Valentine.

  ◆full of money は直前の safes を修飾している。
  ◆to hear は「感情が起こった原因」を表す to-不定詞の副詞用法。「that-節の内容を聞いてうれしく 思った」という意味。
  訳：--

⑫ Jimmy, / looking like an athletic young man just home from college, / walked down the street toward the hotel.

(S ... V 表示付き)

  ◆looking … の分詞構文が挿入されている。主語は Jimmy，動詞は walked。
  ◆walked down の down は必ずしも下に向かって進むわけではなく，単に遠ざかることを表す。
  訳：--

Part 2 教科書 p.152〜p.153 ◁意味のまとまりに注意して，本文全体を聞こう。 ◎2-44

①Jimmy saw a boy / playing on the steps / of the bank / and began asking him questions / about the town. // ②After a time, / the young lady came out of the bank. // ③This time / she pretended / not to notice the young man / with the suitcase, / and went her way. // ④"Isn't that young lady Polly Simpson?" / Jimmy asked the boy. //

⑤"No," / answered the boy. // ⑥"She's Annabel Adams. // ⑦Her father is the owner / of this bank." //

⑧Jimmy went to the hotel. // ⑨He told the hotel clerk / that his name was Ralph D. Spencer, / and that he had come / to Elmore / to look for a place / where he could set up a shoe shop. // ⑩The clerk was so impressed / by Jimmy's clothes and manner / that he kindly gave him as much information / about the town / as he could. // ⑪Yes, / Elmore needed a good shoe shop. // ⑫It was a pleasant town / to live in, / and the people were friendly. //

⑬"Mr. Spencer" told the hotel clerk / that he would like to stay / in the town / for a few days / and look over the situation. // ⑭Mr. Ralph D. Spencer, / Jimmy Valentine's new identity / —— an identity / created by a sudden attack of love / —— remained in Elmore / and opened a shoe shop. //

⑮Soon / his shoe shop was doing a good business, / and he won the respect / of the community. // ⑯And more importantly, / he got to know Annabel Adams. // ⑰They fell deeply in love / and started / to plan their wedding. //

◁意味のまとまりに注意して，本文全体を音読しよう。 (239 Words)

Words and Phrases 新出単語・表現の意味を調べよう			
after a time	1.	pretend 動 [prɪténd] A2	2.
go one's way	3.	Polly Simpson [pá(:)li sím(p)s(ə)n]	ポリー・シンプソン
Annabel Adams [ǽnəbel ǽdəmz]	アナベル・アダムズ	Ralph D. Spencer [rǽlf díː spénsər]	ラルフ・D・スペンサー
set up ...	4.	manner 名 [mǽnər] A2	5.
as ... as one can	6.	pleasant 形 [pléz(ə)nt] A2	7.

| identity 图 [aɪdéntəti] B1 | 8. | more importantly | 9. |
| get to ～ | 10. | wedding 图 [wédɪŋ] A2 | 11. |

A 【Comprehension 1】 Fill in the blanks in Japanese.

パラグラフごとの要点を整理しよう【思考力・判断力・表現力】

ジミー・バレンタイン	・若い女性はアナベル・アダムズという名前だと知る。 ・ラルフ・D・スペンサーと名乗り，エルモアのホテルに滞在。ホテルのフロント係からこの町の（1.　　　）を聞き出す。 ・エルモアで（2.　　　）を開き，繁盛店となる。地域の人にも受け入れられる。
アナベル・アダムズ	・エルモア銀行のオーナーの（3.　　　）である。
⇒ジミーとアナベルは知り合う。愛し合うようになり，（4.　　　）の準備を始める。		

B 【Comprehension 2】 Answer the following questions in English.

本文のポイントについて答えよう【思考力・判断力・表現力】

1. Why did Jimmy ask the boy if the young lady was Polly Simpson?

----

2. Why did Jimmy win the respect of the community?

C 【Key Sentences】 Translate the following sentences.

重要文について確認しよう【知識・技能】【思考力・判断力・表現力】

　　　　　S　　V　　O　　C　　　　　　　　　　　　　　　　　　V　　　O
① Jimmy saw a boy playing on the steps of the bank and began asking him questions about the town.

◆前半は S＋V＋O＋C（＝現在分詞）になっている。see＋O＋～ing で「O が～しているのを見る」の意味。
◆後半は （S＋）V＋O（＝動名詞）になっている。begin ～ing は「～し始める」の意味。動名詞 asking に，さらに目的語が 2 つ（him, questions about …）続いている。

訳：--------

⑭ Mr. Ralph D. Spencer, / Jimmy Valentine's new identity ─── an identity created by a sudden attack of love ─── / remained in Elmore and opened a shoe shop.

◆ Mr. Ralph D. Spencer と Jimmy Valentine's new identity は同格の関係であり，その後のダッシュにはさまれた部分が new identity の説明を加えている。
◆述語動詞は remained と opened の 2 つが and で並列されている。

訳：--------

Part 3　教科書 p.154〜p.155　📢意味のまとまりに注意して，本文全体を聞こう。 ⊚2-46

①One day, / Jimmy wrote a letter / to one of his old friends / in Little Rock. // ②The letter said, / "I want / to give you my tools. // ③You couldn't buy them / even for a thousand dollars. // ④I don't need them anymore / because I finished with the old business / a year ago. // ⑤I will never touch another man's money / again." //

⑥It was a few days / after Jimmy sent his letter / that Ben Price secretly arrived / in Elmore. // ⑦He went around the town / in his quiet way / until he found out all / he wanted to know. // ⑧From a drugstore / across the street / from Spencer's shoe shop, / he watched Ralph D. Spencer / walk by. // ⑨"You think / you're going to marry the banker's daughter, / don't you, / Jimmy?" / said Ben / to himself, / softly. // ⑩"Well, / I'm not so sure / about that!" //

⑪The next morning, / Jimmy had breakfast / at the Adams home. // ⑫That day, / he was going to Little Rock / to order his wedding suit, / buy something nice / for Annabel, / and give his tools away / to his friend. //

⑬After breakfast, / several members / of the Adams family / went to the bank together / —— Mr. Adams, / Annabel, / Jimmy, / and Annabel's married sister / with her two little girls, / aged five and nine. // ⑭On the way to the bank, / they waited / outside Jimmy's shop / while he ran up to his room / and got his suitcase. // ⑮Then / they went on / to the bank. //

📢意味のまとまりに注意して，本文全体を音読しよう。(228 Words)

Words and Phrases	新出単語・表現の意味を調べよう		
Little Rock [lít(ə)lrὰ(:)k]	リトルロック	finish with …	1.
go around …	2.	find out …	3.
walk by	4.	banker 图 [bǽŋkər] B2	5.
say to oneself	6.	be sure about …	7.
go on to …	8.		

A 【Comprehension 1】 Fill in the blanks in Japanese.

パラグラフごとの要点を整理しよう【思考力・判断力・表現力】

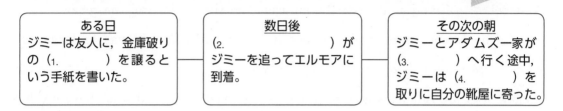

ある日	数日後	その次の朝
ジミーは友人に，金庫破りの（1.　　　）を譲るという手紙を書いた。	（2.　　　　　　　）がジミーを追ってエルモアに到着。	ジミーとアダムズ一家が（3.　　　）へ行く途中，ジミーは（4.　　　）を取りに自分の靴屋に寄った。

B 【Comprehension 2】 Answer the following questions in English.

本文のポイントについて答えよう【思考力・判断力・表現力】

1. Why did Jimmy write a letter to one of his old friends?

    ----

2. Why did Ben Price say that he was not so sure about Jimmy's marriage?

    ----

3. On the way to the bank, what did Jimmy do in his shop?

C 【Key Sentences】 Fill in the blank and translate the following sentences.

重要文について確認しよう【知識・技能】【思考力・判断力・表現力】

③ You couldn't buy them even for a thousand dollars.

  ◆ them＝my（1.　　　[英語で]）。

  訳：--

⑥ **It was** a few days after Jimmy sent his letter **that** Ben Price secretly arrived in Elmore.

  ◆ It was … that ～は強調構文と呼ばれるもので，「～なのは…だった」と，「…」の内容を前に出して強調する。この文では，時を表す副詞句が強調されている。

  訳：--

⑧ From a drugstore across the street from Spencer's shoe shop, <u>he</u> <u>watched</u>
_S　_V
<u>Ralph D. Spencer</u> <u>walk</u> by.
_O　_C

  ◆ S＋V（＝知覚動詞）＋O＋C（＝原形不定詞）の文。watch＋O＋C で「Oが～するのを見る」の意味。

  訳：--

Part 4 教科書 p.156〜p.157 📢意味のまとまりに注意して，本文全体を聞こう。 💿2-48

① They all went into the banking-room / ── Jimmy, / too, / for Mr. Adams' future son-in-law / was welcome / anywhere. // ② Everyone in the bank / was glad / to see the good-looking, nice young man / who was going to marry Annabel. // ③ Jimmy put down the suitcase / in the corner / of the room. //

④ The Elmore Bank had just put in a new safe. // ⑤ It was as large as a small room / and it had a very special new kind of door / that was controlled / by a clock. // ⑥ Mr. Adams was very proud of this new safe / and was showing / how to set the time / when the door should open. // ⑦ The two children, / May and Agatha, / enjoyed touching all the interesting parts / of its shining heavy door. //

⑧ While these things were happening, / Ben Price quietly entered the bank / and looked inside the banking-room. // ⑨ He told the bank teller / that he didn't want anything; / he was just waiting / for a man / he knew. //

⑩ Suddenly, / there were screams / from the women. // ⑪ May, / the five-year-old girl, / had firmly closed the door / of the safe / by accident, / and Agatha was inside! // ⑫ Mr. Adams tried hard / to pull open the door / for a moment, / and then cried, / "The door can't be opened! // ⑬ And the clock / ── I haven't started it / yet." //

⑭ "Please break it open!" / Agatha's mother cried out. //

⑮ "Quiet!" / said Mr. Adams, / raising a shaking hand. // ⑯ "Everyone, / be quiet / for a moment. // ⑰ Agatha!" / he called as loudly / as he could. // ⑱ "Can you hear me?" // ⑲ They could hear, / although not clearly, / the sound / of the child's voice. // ⑳ In the darkness / inside the safe, / she was screaming / with fear. // ㉑ Agatha's mother, / now getting more desperate, / started hitting the door / with her hands. // 📢意味のまとまりに注意して，本文全体を音読しよう。(277 Words)

Words and Phrases 新出単語・表現の意味を調べよう			
banking 名[bǽŋkɪŋ] A2	1.	son-in-low 名[sʌ́nɪnlɔ̀ː] B2	2.
good-looking 形 [gʊ̀dlʊ́kɪŋ] A2	3.	put down …	4.

put in …	5.	be proud of …	6.
Agatha [ǽgəθə]	アガサ	teller 名[télər] B1	7.
scream 名[skríːm] A2	8.	firmly 副[fə́ːrmli] B1	9.
by accident	10.	pull open …	11.
for a moment	12.	cry out	13.
darkness 名[dáːrknəs] B1	14.	fear 名[fíər] A2	15.
desperate 形 [désp(ə)rət] B1	16.		

A 【Comprehension 1】 Fill in the blanks in Japanese.

パラグラフごとの要点を整理しよう【思考力・判断力・表現力】

ジミー・バレンタイン (1.　　　　　　　　　　　　) を執務室の隅のほうに置く。	アダムズ氏 (2.　　　) で制御する最新型の金庫を紹介する。
銀行の執務室での出来事	
ベン・プライス 銀行に入り，(3.　　　) 内の様子を伺う。	アナベルの姉の娘 メイが誤って金庫の扉を閉めてしまい，(4.　　　) が金庫の中に閉じ込められてしまう。

B 【Comprehension 2】 Answer the following questions in English.

本文のポイントについて答えよう【思考力・判断力・表現力】

1. What had the Elmore Bank just put in?

----

2. Why did Mr. Adams say "Quiet!" ?

C 【Key Sentence】 Fill in the blank and translate the following sentence.

重要文について確認しよう【知識・技能】【思考力・判断力・表現力】

⑲ They <u>could hear</u>, / although not clearly, / <u>the sound of the child's voice</u>.
  S V   O

◆although not clearly という副詞節が文中に挿入されている。
　省略を補うと although they could not (1.　　　[英語で]) clearly となる。

訳 : ----

101

Part 5 教科書 p.158～p.159 🔊意味のまとまりに注意して，本文全体を聞こう。 ◎2-50

①Annabel turned to Jimmy. // ②Her large eyes were full of pain, / but not yet despairing. // ③A woman believes / that the man / she loves / can find a way / to do anything. // ④"Can't you do something, / Ralph? // ⑤Try, / won't you?" // ⑥He looked at her / with a strange, soft smile / on his lips / and in his eyes. //

⑦"Annabel," / he said, / "give me that rose / you are wearing, / will you?" //

⑧She couldn't understand / what he meant, / but she put the rose / in his hand. // ⑨Jimmy took it / and placed it / in the pocket / of his vest. // ⑩Then / he threw off his coat. // ⑪With that act, / Ralph D. Spencer disappeared, / and Jimmy Valentine took his place. // ⑫"Stay away from the door, / all of you," / he ordered. //

⑬He placed his suitcase / on the table / and opened it. // ⑭From that time on, / he didn't pay any attention / to anyone else there. // ⑮Quickly / he laid the strange shining tools / on the table. // ⑯Nobody moved / as they watched him work. // ⑰Soon / Jimmy's drill was biting smoothly / into the steel door. // ⑱In ten minutes / —— faster / than he had ever done it before / —— he opened the door. //

⑲Agatha, / completely exhausted / but unharmed, / ran into her mother's arms. // ⑳Jimmy Valentine silently put his coat back on / and walked / toward the front door / of the bank. // ㉑As he went, / he thought / he heard a voice call, / "Ralph!" // ㉒But he never hesitated. // ㉓At the door, / a big man was standing / in his way. // ㉔"Hello, / Ben!" / said Jimmy. // ㉕"You're here / at last, / aren't you? // ㉖Well, / let's go. // ㉗I don't care now." //

㉘"I'm afraid / you're mistaken, / Mr. Spencer," / said Ben Price. // ㉙"I don't believe / I recognize you." // ㉚Then / the big detective turned away / and walked slowly down the street. // 🔊意味のまとまりに注意して，本文全体を音読しよう。(283 Words)

Words and Phrases	新出単語・表現の意味を調べよう		
turn to ...	1.	despairing 形 [dɪspéərɪŋ]	2.
vest 名 [vést]	3.	throw off ...	4.

take one's place	5.	stay away from …	6.
from that time on	7.	pay attention to …	8.
smoothly 副 [smúːðli] A2	9.	steel 名 [stíːl] B1	10.
exhausted 形 [ɪɡzɔ́ːstɪd] B1	11.	unharmed 形 [ʌnhɑ́ːrmd] B1	12.
run into …	13.	put … on	14.
hesitate 動 [hézɪtèɪt] B1	15.	in one's way	16.
at last	17.	recognize 動 [rékəɡnàɪz] B1	18.
turn away	19.		

A 【Comprehension 1】 Fill in the blanks in Japanese.

要点を整理しよう【思考力・判断力・表現力】

- (1.　　　　) がジミーに助けを求めた。
- ジミーは (2.　　　　) を脱いで，道具を取り出した。
- (3.　　　　) の扉を開け，アガサを助け出した。
- ジミーはその場を立ち去ろうと玄関に向かった。
- 逮捕される覚悟をしたが，ベン・プライスはジミーに (4.　　　　) ふりをして去っていった。

B 【Comprehension 2】 Answer the following questions in English.

本文のポイントについて答えよう【思考力・判断力・表現力】

1. What was inside Jimmy's suitcase?

----

2. How long did it take Jimmy to open the door of the safe?

C 【Key Sentence】 Fill in the blank and translate the following sentence.

重要文について確認しよう【知識・技能】【思考力・判断力・表現力】

⑪ With that act, Ralph D. Spencer disappeared, and Jimmy Valentine took his place.

◆ that act とは，ジミーが (1.　　　　　　　　　[日本語で]) ことを指す。

訳: --

103